Contents

WE were about to go to press with this month's issue of JOHNSTONE, with Assange on the front cover, when the situation in Gaza blew up and just like that we couldn't possibly lede with anything else. Turn to page three for our Notes From The Edge Of The Narrative Matrix version of the unfolding events in the Palestine-Israel conflict.

We also examine the burgeoning popularity of the word "unprovoked" both in Ukraine (p60) and Israel (p70); the great argument for revolution a wealthy capitalist accidentally made (p14); and the island calling into question whether the US gains enthusiastic consent for inserting its military bases into foreign countries (p23).

All works are written by Caitlin Johnstone and Tim Foley. The Caitlin Johnstone project is 100 percent reader-funded.

The Israel–Palestine Issue Is Not Complicated
And Other Notes From The Edge Of The Narrative Matrix

The Israel-Palestine issue is not complicated; an apartheid regime abuses and oppresses an indigenous ethnic group who don't have the same rights as others. The only reason anyone thinks it's complicated is because they assume if it were simple, the news would've told them so.

Really Israel-Palestine is one of the easier conflicts to understand on the world stage; conflicts like Ukraine or Syria are much more complicated. It's obvious at a glance that there's one group in power and another group being treated very badly by that group, but because the press frames it as a complicated issue with its sympathies wildly slanted toward the apartheid regime, people assume it can't be as simple as what it looks like at first glance.

It is, though. Israel is exactly the abusive apartheid regime it looks like on the surface. Remember this as the bodies pile up and Gaza is turned into a smoldering crater. This is exactly what it looks like.

The coming days are going to be full of western news media slyly reversing the aggressor-defender relationship and reporting as though all the violence began with the Hamas offensive, spontaneously out of nowhere.

.

The problem with oppressing a population with maximum force is that at some point they start figuring they've got nothing to lose by fighting back.

.

Do I think this latest uprising will end in more positive results than negative for Palestinians? No. Does that mean I'll condemn the Palestinian resistance for fighting back? Also no.

This is because doing so would be nonsensical, for a couple of different reasons. Firstly, because nobody can tell me what the Palestinians should do instead that is both realistic and reasonable. It would be easy for me to sit here in my armchair and say the Palestinians should either maintain the status quo or lie down, relinquish their homes and homeland and accept whatever table scraps they're able to get, but we can see from the Palestinian perspective that that's not reasonable. It would be easy for me to sit in my armchair and argue that Palestinians should just focus on securing a one-state or two-state solution, but we can see from the Israeli political landscape that that's not realistic.

So what else can they do? What reasonable and realistic options do they have? No one can provide me a satisfactory answer.

Secondly, it would be nonsensical for me to condemn the actions of Hamas on the grounds that it will make things worse for the Palestinians because the fact that Israel always responds to Palestinian resistance by killing a lot of Palestinians is itself a very concrete manifestation of the abuses the Palestinians are resisting. It would not be legitimate for me to sit in my armchair and tell someone to stop resisting their abuser just because it will cause them to receive more abuse; that's not a valid reason to condemn resistance.

Ultimately this is just Palestinians doing what they feel they need to do out of total desperation, because they feel backed into a corner with no other options. And they feel backed into a corner with no other options because that does appear to be the case. There are a lot of people I could blame for their being in those circumstances, but the very last on that list would be the victims of the abuse themselves.

.

Israel apologists will brand anyone who criticizes Israel an anti-semite while adamantly denying that they include "criticizing Israel" in their definition of anti-semitism. If you ask them to name a forceful and sustained critic of Israel's abuses who is not an anti-semite they generally won't be able to, because they absolutely do regard all critics of Israel as anti-semites, but they can't admit that they do this because they know the public is catching on to this tactic and they know it hurts their propaganda efforts.

In this way they're exactly the same as people who brand all critics of US foreign policy toward Russia as Kremlin propagandists and all critics of US foreign policy toward China as secret agents of "the CCP". Ask anyone who accuses you of being a Kremlin troll for criticizing western proxy warfare in Ukraine to name one forceful and sustained critic of that war who they don't consider a Kremlin operative; they won't be able to. This is because their definition of "Kremlin operative" actually includes "anyone who criticizes US foreign policy toward Russia". But they can't admit this, because they know it makes them look ridiculous.

.

Whenever something like this happens warmongers always seize on the emotional frenzy of the moment to shove through insane acts of warmongering and scream vitriol at anyone who questions them. Then later when all the facts are in people slowly start to realize that something went very wrong, and that they were deceived.

After 9/11 anyone who didn't support multiple full-scale ground invasions of sovereign nations was a terrorist sympathizer and a Saddam apologist. We were told Al Qaeda were evil, irrational actors who attacked because "they hate us for our freedom", and we need to support a war on terror against any nation deemed threatening because all such monsters understand is violence. Now both the Iraq and Afghanistan wars are regarded as colossal mistakes by anyone who's honest.

When Russia invaded Ukraine anyone who wanted peace talks instead of a

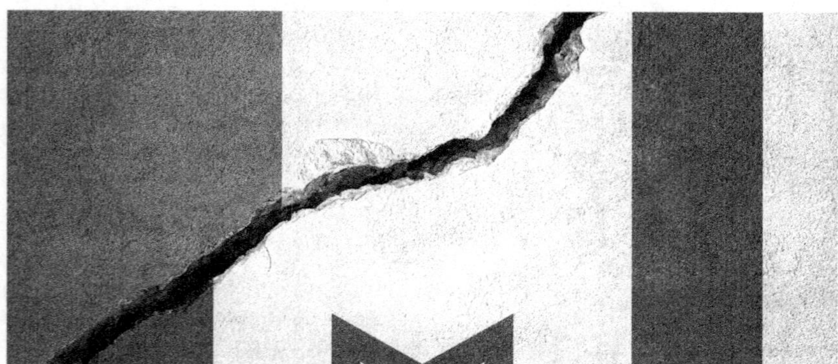

rapidly escalating proxy war between nuclear-armed nations was a Putin lover and a Kremlin shill. We were told Putin invaded solely because he is evil and hates freedom, and we need to support a war against him because all such monsters understand is violence. Now the counteroffensive failed, the US is having trouble getting proxy war funding through congress, and even the head of NATO acknowledges that this war was provoked by NATO expansion.

And now we're facing another instance of intense emotional frenzy, and we're being told that Hamas attacked Israel completely unprovoked for no other reason than because they are evil monsters who love killing Jews. We will be told to support any act of war deemed necessary, because all such monsters understand is violence.

Someday we're going to have to stop falling for this tired old song and dance.

·

The western press are largely to blame for all this. If they'd just told the truth instead of running "Palestinian child walks into bullet" headlines this whole time and telling everyone that boycotting Israel is genocide, political pressure could've long ago been brought about to force a peaceful and just resolution to this mess.

If they'd just done their jobs and reported the facts to the public, there never would've been enough public consent for the US empire to back a brutal apartheid regime which cannot exist without nonstop violence, and peaceful resolutions would've become unavoidable.

Instead they hid all those abuses from the public for generations, creating an environment where peaceful resolutions are impossible and giving rise to Palestinian factions which understandably see violent force as the only viable answer.

This is their fault. They created this mess with a mountain of lies and obfuscation, and now those lies are being paid for with rivers of blood. The western press are war criminals. They've committed crimes against humanity.

·

Israel apologists will seriously be like, "Why is everyone so obsessed with the nuclear-armed colonialist apartheid state which plays a pivotal role in US warmongering in the middle east? The only possible explanation is that they all harbor some weird hatred of Jewish people!"

·

It's getting harder and harder to argue that the US-led world order brings more peace and stability to the world than the war and instability it causes. As more and more force is brought to bear against nations and groups who refuse to submit to Washington's dictates, we're seeing more and more conflict and chaos. Russia's refusal to lie down before Washington resulted in the Ukraine war and all the nuclear brinkmanship that comes with it. Hamas, Hezbollah, Ansarallah, Syria and Iran refusing to

prostrate themselves to the US power alliance results in constant violence in the middle east. As the imperial crosshairs move to Beijing we're now faced with the terrifying prospect of a hot war with China.

At a certain point you have to ask, if the US-led world order requires more and more violence and nuclear brinkmanship to maintain, what specifically is the argument for maintaining it in the first place? Does it not at some point begin to cease looking like "order" at all, and instead like a tyrannical empire trying to rule the world no matter how much death and destruction is necessary to subjugate it?

·

Israeli defense minister Yoav Gallant has announced a "complete siege" of all of Gaza in response to the Hamas attack on Saturday, justifying the deliberate targeting of civilians with siege warfare by the claim that Israel is at war with "human animals".

"I have ordered a complete siege on the Gaza Strip. There will be no electricity, no food, no fuel, everything is closed," Gallant said Monday, adding, "We are fighting human animals and we are acting accordingly."

So there you have it, folks: they're attacking civilians, which is fine, because they're not actually attacking human beings.

There it is. The true face of Israel, naked and unadorned in the cold light of day. The mask is completely off now.

Israel apologists get mad at me for criticizing Israel, when Israeli officials are saying much worse things with their own mouths about what Israel is than I ever have.

·

Suspicions that the Saturday attack was allowed to happen have been given more weight by an

Associated Press report which cites an anonymous Egyptian intelligence official saying Egypt had warned Israel "something big" was in the works in advance of the attacks.

"We have warned them an explosion of the situation is coming, and very soon, and it would be big. But they underestimated such warnings," the official said.•

Multiple US officials have deleted tweets calling for ceasefire negotiations to end the conflict. Secretary of State Tony Blinken and the Twitter account for the US Office of Palestinian Affairs both removed posts from the platform, the former calling for ceasefire mediation from Türkiye and the latter urging "all sides to refrain from violence and retaliatory attacks." The exact reasons for the deletion are unknown, but the general reasons are politically obvious.

.

Prominent figures have been referring to the Saturday attacks as "Israel's 9/11", which should set off immediate alarm bells in everyone's head. The most significant thing that happened on September 11th 2001 was not the three thousand deaths from the attacks themselves, but the dawn of a new age of western interventionism and military expansionism that would go on to kill orders of magnitude more people than died on 9/11.

That's what you should think about when people begin comparing a new event to 9/11: not to the event itself, but to the mountains of unwise decisions of far greater consequence that were made in its wake. That should be an automatic association in our minds. We should become more skeptical and oppositional toward the warmongering agendas of our government and its allies when we hear things compared to 9/11, not less.

.

It's hilarious that it's 2023 and people still think calling you a terrorist defender and an anti-semite will stop you from criticizing the abuses of a nation which all leading human rights organizations have now labeled an apartheid state.

.

I built a new house. There were people living where I wanted to build it so I just started building it on top of them. They tried to stop me so I had to kill them for being terrorists. If you disagree with my actions you're basically a Nazi. I have a right to defend my house.

.

Following the discourse on all this has been a good reminder of why you shouldn't take the "anti-war" posturing of MAGA Republicans seriously. They're fully on-board with a ton of warmongering agendas against Palestinians, Iran, China, and socialist governments in Latin America; they're just anti Democrat wars.

.

A nation that cannot exist without nonstop war is not a nation at all—it's an ongoing military operation.

A nation that can't exist without nonstop war is like a house that can't stand without nonstop construction. If I lived in a house that was constantly full of construction workers and the sounds of construction equipment 24/7/365 because if they stopped working on it it would collapse, eventually I'd figure I need to either (A) change the kind of house I'm trying to build, or (B) build somewhere else.

If I was an Israel supporter I'd be thinking very carefully about the things I'm posting online in the build-up to what could end up being regarded as one of history's worst genocidal massacres. The internet doesn't forget. What you're tweeting today could haunt you for life.

.

Killing civilians with military explosives is not actually any more humane or civilized than killing them with firearms. They'll cause gruesome injuries and slow, excruciating deaths by suffocation, burns and body trauma. They're horrific weapons of mass murder.

The one and only reason you don't see as much shock and horror in response to killing with military explosives as killing with firearms is because killing with military explosives is something you do from far away. When they show video clips of the buildings getting blown up, you're not seeing the people being crushed to death underneath them and ripped apart in the blasts. It's just a fun little sanitized clip of an explosion, like you're watching an action movie or playing a video game.

It's not actually any nicer than if the IDF were running around shooting civilians with rifles or running them through with swords, it's just more detached, so it lets people psychologically compartmentalize away from what's really happening.

That's what so much perception management is about with the US and its allies these days; helping the public compartmentalize away from the horrors their side is unleashing upon the world. They do it with their propaganda, their lies by omission and their "Palestinian child walks into bullet" headlines, they do it with the uniform "unprovoked act of terror" statements by their government officials, and they do it by the actual ways in which they conduct their acts of mass murder.

It's all about sedating the public to sleep and never startling them into a wakeful recognition of the ghastly things that are being done with the support of their government.

.

Cutting off Gaza's electricity doesn't just hurt the civilians who live there, it greatly hampers the world's visibility into what's happening in there. Think how much harder it's going to be for people in Gaza to record and upload video footage to the internet now.

And that of course entirely by design. Israel has every incentive to impede visibility into its abuses, and it always has; that's why it has an extensive track record of targeting and threatening journalists and media outlets.

.

Seeing a lot of dubiously sourced and flat-out unevidenced claims about about Hamas fighters decapitating babies and committing mass rapes that look a lot like atrocity propaganda, which as we were reminded in Ukraine is very common in wartime. Mass media employees learned in Ukraine that they can parrot any amount of atrocity propaganda during a war without any professional consequences so long as it comes from the side their government is on. Read the news very critically.

.

It's important to understand how completely un-monolithic Jews are on the issue of Israel and Zionism. The fiercest and most incisive critics of Israel I follow are all Jewish. Don't let propagandists frame this as "Jew haters vs Jews" when it's really justice vs injustice.

.

It's not about hypocrisy. The point of highlighting the contradiction in supporting both Ukraine and Israel is to show that western imperialists do not actually stand for what they claim to stand for, and that their entire framing of where they stand in these conflicts is a lie.

Supporting one group that's fighting a hostile occupation and opposing another that's doing the same would only be hypocritical if your support really was based on opposing occupiers and supporting people's right to self-determination. Supporting one group that's full of neo-Nazis who hate Jews while supporting another in the name of protecting Jewish people would only be hypocritical if your support actually had anything to do with protecting religious minorities.

In reality the empire just supports who it supports because that's where its interests happen to be advanced in each instance. Having Ukraine as a proxy advances US strategic interests against Russia and having Israel as a proxy advances US strategic interests against Iran and Syria. They're not hypocritical at all; they're perfectly consistent. They're grabbing power and control in whatever way's most convenient, in perfect alignment with their actual values.

To be a hypocrite is no great evil in and of itself; we're all a bit hypocritical in some ways. What absolutely is a great evil is inflicting violence and destruction throughout the world in order to pursue planetary hegemony while lying about your reasons for doing so.

That's why we highlight the contradictions. Not to show that the empire and its supporters are hypocrites, but to show the far greater evils hidden behind those contradictions.

Images by Adobe Stock

NATO Chief Openly Admits Russia Invaded Ukraine Because Of NATO Expansion

During a speech at the EU Parliament's foreign affairs committee on Thursday, NATO Secretary General Jens Stoltenberg clearly and repeatedly acknowledged that Putin made the decision to invade Ukraine because of fears of NATO expansionism.

His comments, initially flagged by journalist Thomas Fazi, read as follows:

> The background was that President Putin declared in the autumn of 2021, and actually sent a draft treaty that they wanted NATO to sign, to promise no more NATO enlargement. That was what he sent us. And was a pre-condition for not invade Ukraine. Of course we didn't sign that.

> The opposite happened. He wanted us to sign that promise, never to enlarge NATO. He wanted us to remove our military infrastructure in all Allies that have joined NATO since 1997, meaning half of NATO, all the Central and Eastern Europe, we should remove NATO from that part of our Alliance, introducing some kind of B, or second class membership. We rejected that.

> So he went to war to prevent NATO, more NATO, close to his borders.

Stoltenberg made these remarks as part of a general gloat about the fact that Putin invaded Ukraine to prevent NATO expansion and yet the invasion has resulted in Sweden and Finland applying to join the alliance, saying it "demonstrates that when President Putin invaded a European country to prevent more NATO, he's getting the exact opposite."

Stoltenberg's remarks would probably have been classified as Russian propaganda by plutocrat-funded "disinformation experts" and imperial "fact checkers" if it had been said online by someone like you or me, but because it came from the head of NATO as part of a screed against the Russian president it's been allowed to pass through without objection.

In reality Stoltenberg is just stating a well-established fact: contrary to the official western narrative, Putin invaded Ukraine not because he is evil and hates freedom but because no great power ever allows foreign military threats to amass on its borders — including the United States. That's why so many western analysts and officials spent years warning that NATO's actions were going to provoke a war, and yet when war broke out we were slammed with a tsunami of mass media propaganda repeating over and over and over again that this was an "unprovoked invasion".

It would have been so very, very easy to prevent this horrific war. Off-ramp after off-ramp after off-ramp was passed to get us to where we're at now. Chance after chance after chance to avoid all this pointless death and misery was passed up, both before 2014 and every year since. The US-centralized power structure knowingly chose this war, and it did so to advance its own interests. If people really, deeply understood this, the entire western empire would collapse.

It's the damnedest thing how you'll get called a Kremlin agent for saying that this war was provoked by NATO expansionism and that it serves US interests, even when NATO openly says this war was provoked by NATO expansionism and US officials keep openly saying that this war serves US interests.

The latest entry in the latter category came in the form of a Thursday tweet by Senate Minority Leader Mitch McConnell, which reads, "Standing with our allies against Russian aggression isn't charity. In fact—it's a direct investment in replenishing America's arsenal with American weapons built by American workers. Expanding our defense industrial base puts America in a stronger position to out-compete China."

When official authorized narrative-makers acknowledge these things it's okay, but when normal human beings do it it's Kremlin disinformation. This is because when the authorized narrative-makers do it they're doing it to advance the information interests of the US empire—to explain to war-weary Americans how this war benefits their country, or to mock Putin's failure to stop the enlargement of NATO—whereas when normal people do it it's to establish what's true and factual.

This all happens as a study sponsored by the EU with a group funded by US oligarch Pierre Omidyar is being circulated by mass media outlets like The Washington Post finding that Twitter under Elon Musk has not been doing enough to censor "Russian propaganda" on the platform. This would put Musk in violation of the European Union's Digital Services Act, which requires platforms to restrict such materials.

As Glenn Greenwald has noted, the Digital Services Act defines "Russian propaganda" so extremely broadly that it includes "ideological alignment with the Russian state" in the category of materials that must be censored, which includes people who "parrot the Kremlin's narratives through originally produced content or by spreading Kremlin aligned narratives to different target audiences and languages."

Anyone who speaks out against US foreign policy relating to Russia online is always immediately accused of "parroting Kremlin narratives" by empire apologists mindlessly regurgitating what they've been told to believe by outlets like The Washington Post, whether they have anything to do with the Russian government or not. I myself have no affiliation or interaction with the Russian state whatsoever, yet I receive many of these accusations every single day online just for criticizing US foreign policy.

If I were the NATO Secretary General publicly gloating about how Putin's efforts to stop the expansion of NATO have failed, it would be fine for me to acknowledge that NATO expansion provoked this war after our refusal to prevent a needless conflict. But because I am harming the information interests of the western empire instead of helping them, that makes me a Russian propagandist.

This isn't because the definition of "Russian propaganda" is flawed, but because it is working exactly as intended. The push to marginalize and eliminate "Russian propaganda" has never had anything to do with fighting the actual materials put out by the Russian state (which have essentially zero meaningful existence in the western world); the push has always been about stomping out opposition to US foreign policy.

Like so much else in this world when examining the behavior of power, it's ultimately all about narrative control. The powerful understand that whoever controls the dominant narrative about world events actually controls the world, because real power isn't just controlling what happens but controlling what people think about what happens. That's the real glue holding the US-centralized empire together, and the world will never have a chance at knowing peace until people start bringing consciousness to it.

Featured image via the European Parliament.

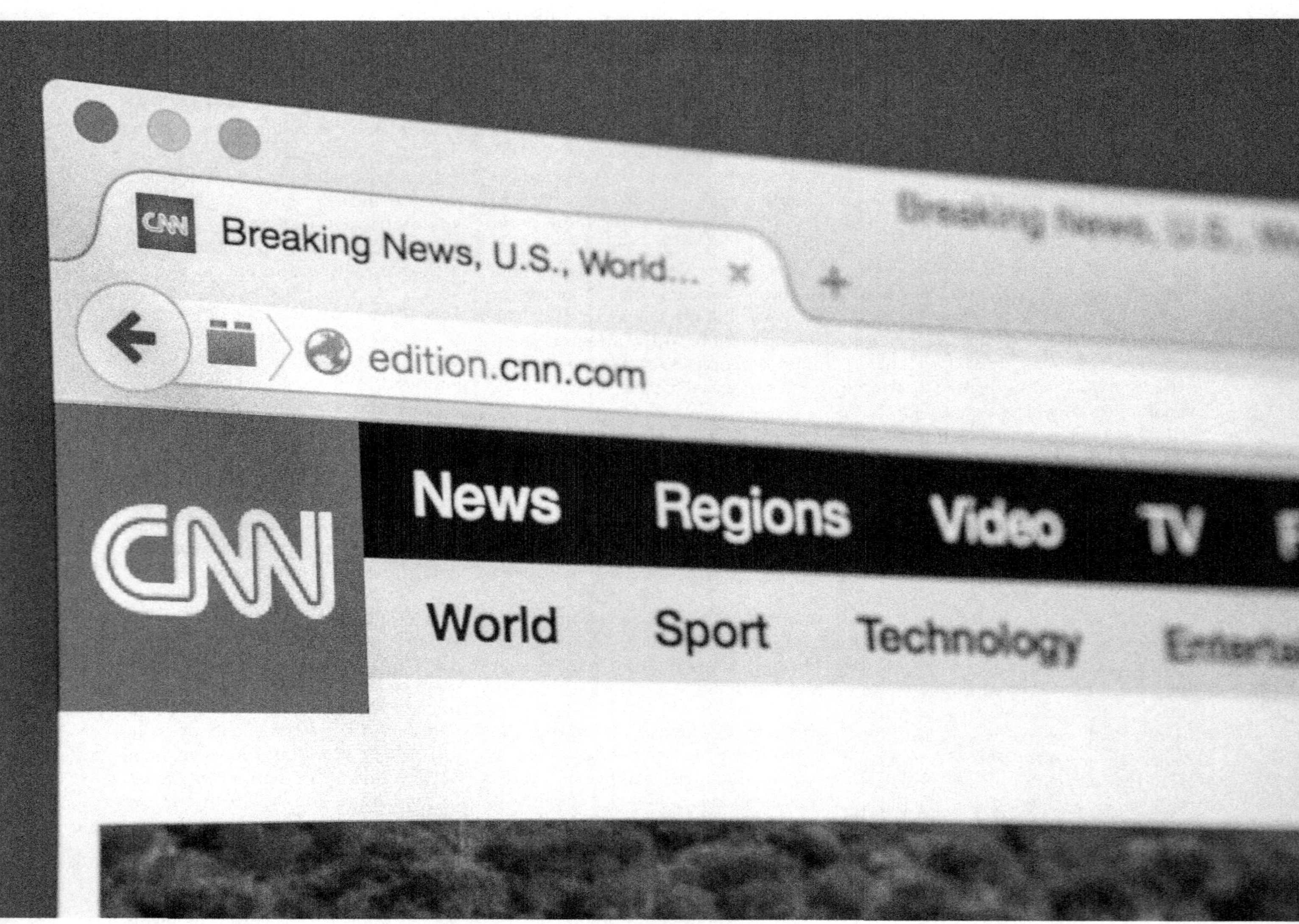

The Top Ten Dumbest Things Empire Propagandists Ask Us To Believe

When you live under an empire that's held together by lies, you'll be asked to believe a lot of intensely stupid bullshit. Here are the top ten dumbest things the propagandists of the US-centralized empire try to get us to swallow.

1. That the US war machine has been surrounding its top two rivals China and Russia with war machinery as an act of defense, rather than an extremely provocative act of aggression.

2. That the war in Ukraine simultaneously (A) was completely unprovoked, and (B) just coincidentally happens to massively advance US strategic interests and therefore should be funded as much as possible.

3. That, okay, all those other wars were based on lies and resulted in disaster, but that couldn't possibly be the case for this current war.

4. That your country's foreign policy is determined by your official elected government, even though the foreign policy remains the same regardless of who is in office.

5. That it is only by pure coincidence that your nation's population remains in a perpetual 50–50 deadlock which prevents anyone's votes from changing the status quo, and the status quo just happens to be perpetually frozen along lines that hugely advantage the rich and powerful.

6. That the only reason anyone could possibly be critical of the most dangerous impulses of the world's most powerful and destructive government is if they are a secret agent working for the enemies of that government.

7. That the western empire which spent the last two decades murdering Muslims in the Middle East suddenly cares very deeply about the Muslims in China.

8. That Putin invaded Ukraine solely because he is evil and hates freedom, and that the empire is pouring weapons into Ukraine because it loves Ukrainians and wants to protect their freedom and democracy.

9. That foreign propaganda and influence operations are significantly manipulating the way westerners think and vote, but the plutocrats who fully control all the most influential platforms in the western world are not.

10. That we need to be worrying about tyrannical enemies in Beijing and Moscow, instead of tyrannical enemies a lot closer to home.

Pay Attention To The Everyday Horrors

Have you ever noticed how the criticisms that both mainstream US political factions make about their opposition tend to be cartoonish exaggerations and whole cloth lies with little or no grounding in reality?

It's the strangest thing. Since 2015 Democrats have been insisting that Trump's election would spell the end of American democracy and would turn the United States into a Nazi dystopia with goose-stepping brownshirts rounding up minorities for concentration camps. On top of that they began insisting that Trump is a secret agent working for the Kremlin and that Vladimir Putin was secretly operating as the de facto president of the United States.

On the right side of the aisle it's even more ridiculous. They're constantly babbling about a hostile takeover of the United States by socialists and communists, as though the Democrats are anything other than the same garden variety neoliberal capitalists that Republicans are. The more extreme factions prattle on about satanic plots to legalize child molestation, turn children transgender and make everyone eat bugs, which Americans will be powerless to resist because their guns will have been confiscated and their mandatory estrogen jabs will have made them too soft and feminine to fight back.

It's just ridiculously bogus drama queenery from both sides, but they push it anyway, day after day, year after year, each year with more sensationalist melodrama and hyperbole than the year before. They do this for a couple of reasons, the first being that if they started criticizing each other for the actual things they are actually doing, people would start to notice that there's not much meaningful difference between the two parties in terms of actual governance. If Americans started to notice that the US government behaves more or less the same way regardless of which party is in power, the illusion of the two-party puppet show would be shattered, and empire managers would lose a crucial means of social control.

Secondly, both parties criticize each other for fictional offenses because criticizing each other for their actual offenses would draw attention to just how evil they both are in real life. The warmongering. The starvation sanctions. The ecocide. The soaring authoritarianism. Making their citizenry poorer and poorer so their donors can get richer and richer, and then destroying social safety nets and imposing crushing austerity on their poverty-ravaged populace. Facilitating a mind-controlled dystopia in which everyone is brainwashed by propaganda to align their thoughts, speech, labor, actions and votes in accordance with the will of the powerful.

The basic, mundane, ordinary status quo is a waking nightmare that should make us all scream in terror; the only reason we don't is because we don't notice it, and the only reason we don't notice it is because we're used to it. We've never known anything besides this abusive dystopia, so we've got no perspective on what a healthy society would look like and how very, very far we are from it. But if someone was transported from an alternate universe where human civilization was functioning in a healthy way, they would fall to their knees and bawl at what they saw here.

They make up fictional horrors because they don't want you looking at the real ones. They don't want you looking at the suffering of the homeless on the street. At the working poor flailing in endless toil unable to get their heads above water and relax for a minute. At the families in nations like Venezuela, Syria, North Korea and Iran struggling to obtain food and medicine because of imperial economic warfare. At the emaciated bodies of Yemeni children. At the shredded corpses of drone bombing victims. At the inconvenient facts behind the horrors in Ukraine. At Julian Assange languishing in a maximum security prison for the crime of good journalism. At the indoctrinated masses marching blindly to the beat of the imperial drum while being trained to believe they are free. At the biosphere we depend on for survival being poisoned and fed into the machine of global capitalism. At the nuclear holocaust dangling over our heads by an increasingly tenuous thread.

Those are the real horrors. Not the imaginary ones the politicians and propagandists train you to fixate on, but the real ones they train you to overlook. The mundane horrors. The everyday horrors. The horrors we were born into, and got used to over time.

Stop focusing on the threat of some future hypothetical dystopia and pay attention to the dystopia we're living in right now. That's where the real tyranny is at. And that's what the real tyrants work continuously to prevent us from noticing. The more they can keep us shaking our fists at imaginary problems, the longer they can keep us from solving the real ones.

Photo by Adobe Stock

Wealthy Capitalist Accidentally Makes Great Argument For Revolution

Recent comments from a wealthy Australian property developer named Tim Gurner are going viral on social media right now for the unusual frankness with which he discusses the inherent conflicts of interest between the working class and employers, saying workers who've grown lazy and arrogant during Covid need to experience economic pain in the form of unemployment to rein them in and put them in their place.

Gurner, who with a net worth of $912 million is ranked by the Australian Financial Review as the 154th richest person in Australia, made the remarks at the Australian Financial Review Property Summit on Tuesday.

"You know, tradies [Australian slang for tradesmen] have definitely pulled back on productivity," Gurner said. "They have been paid a lot to do not too much in the last few years. And we need to see that change. I think the problem that we've had is that we have people who decided they didn't really want to work so much anymore through Covid."

Gurner continued:

"We need to remind people that they work for the employer, not the other way around. We need to see unemployment rise, unemployment has to jump 40–50 percent. In my view, we need to see pain in the economy. I mean, there's been a systematic change where employees feel the employer is extremely lucky to have them as opposed to the other way around.

"So it's a dynamic that has to change. We've got to kill that attitude and that has to come through hurting the economy which is what the whole global world is trying to do. The governments around the world are trying to increase unemployment, to get that to some sort of normality, and we're seeing it. I think every employer now is seeing it.

"I mean, there are definitely massive layoffs going off and people might not be talking about it, but people are definitely laying people off and we're starting to see less arrogance in the employment market and that has to continue, because that will cascade across the cost balance."

It's not often that you'll see a member of the ruling class reveal their hostile, slave-master attitude toward the working class so transparently. Perhaps Gurner got a little too careless showing off in front of his rich friends at a forum which, like most things that happen in Australia, never attracts much international attention. But it also wouldn't be the first time Gurner drew headlines by publicly expressing his disdain for normal working people; in 2017 he became a meme for blaming the economic struggles of millennials on the idea that they spend too much of their money on avocado toast.

Whether he intended his remarks to gain attention or not, Gurner has gone viral once again, and opponents of the status quo he thrives on are making swift use of his comments.

"I like teaching lefty theory as much as the next guy but I can rarely do better at explaining the connection between capital and social-political domination

than just pointing at what the guys with the capital do and say," reads a popular tweet by Georgetown professor Olúfémi O. Táíwò.

"When Marxists say that capitalism, in order to function, literally requires unemployment and homelessness to discipline wages to ensure satisfactory profitability and maintain a useful social domination of the working class don't take it from us, take it from capitalists," reads another popular share of the Gurner video.

Gurner's statements are unusual in their frankness and in their admission that unemployment is a weapon of the ruling class to bludgeon workers into working harder for less pay, but his push to decrease employment is also entirely in alignment with what influential economists like Larry Summers, Ben Bernanke and Olivier Blanchard have been saying in recent months. Workers making more money is seen by the ruling class as a freakish aberrational problem that needs to be fixed via economic pain instead of a good thing that should be celebrated and normalized.

It's important to remember these frank admissions when they happen, because they don't happen very often. Normally the capitalist class spends its time telling workers they're an important part of the team and we're all family here and hey, have a slice of pizza on us every now and then. But the fact of the matter is that all they really care about is their ability to siphon off the excess value generated by your labor, and they'll come together with remarkable class solidarity to push the state to hurt you financially in order to ensure that they can skim the largest share of that value possible.

This is completely unsustainable. We cannot continue to tolerate systems which must necessarily abuse workers with financial pain in order to keep increasing profits and quarterly statements. We must transcend these competition-based models where people are manipulated by financial pain into stepping on each other's heads in a rat race to show the ruling class that they can generate more profit for their employer than their neighbor can. We need to move into collaboration-based systems in which we all work together for the good of everyone and toward the thriving of our biosphere. Our current status quo systems are choking us to death.

Such changes aren't going to happen until the people start using the power of their numbers to force them to happen. And Tim Gurner just made a splendid argument outlining why this should happen sooner rather than later.

Remember: a class war is already happening. That decision has already been made for us. The only thing we have a say in is whether we fight back or not.

•

☰ 🔍	**FINANCIAL REVIEW**	*Newsfeed* 👤

154	**Tim Gurner**	YoY change **-1.8%**	Wealth **$912m** ⌄

Property developer Tim Gurner's new chain of wellness and anti-ageing gyms, Saint Haven, represent a return to his roots. Gurner's first business was actually a gym, where he worked around the clock to try to get his personal trainer accreditation. He'd sell up and knock on doors to get into the property game, offering to work free to get a foot in the door with Morry Schwartz. Among the big projects he currently has going all along the eastern seaboard is a $1.2 billion build-to-rent development fund in partnership with Qualitas.

Wealth last year **$929m**	Source of wealth **Property**

Putin Doesn't Think US Foreign Policy Will Change If Trump Is Re-Elected (And He's Probably Right)

Vladimir Putin said at the Eastern Economic Forum on Tuesday that he wouldn't expect any meaningful changes in US policy toward Russia if former president Donald Trump secures re-election next year.

TASS reports the following on the Russian president's comments:

"I think there will be no fundamental changes regarding Russia in US foreign policy, no matter who is elected president," Putin said. "Mr. [Donald] Trump (ex-president and Republican Party candidate—TASS) says he will solve acute problems, including the Ukrainian crisis, in a few days, this can only please. Nevertheless, he too imposed sanctions on Russia during his presidency," Putin recalled.

The US, according to the Russian president, "views Russia as a permanent adversary, or even an enemy, and has hammered this into the heads of ordinary Americans." "The current authorities have tuned American society into an anti-Russian vein and spirit—that's what it's all about. They have done it, and now it will be very difficult to somehow turn this ship in the other direction," Putin said.

This is not the first time Putin has made such comments. When Oliver Stone asked him in an interview during Trump's presidency what has changed from administration to administration in the four US presidents he'd gone through during his leadership, Putin replied, "Almost nothing. Your bureaucracy is very strong and it is that bureaucracy that rules the world."

And he's right; from Bush to Obama to Trump to Biden there has been a consistent pattern of escalation which has now culminated in a terrible proxy war—provoked by western actions—which has the potential to go nuclear at any time. Trump has been campaigning on the claim that he can end the Ukraine war in a day if re-elected, but there is no actual reason to believe that's true.

Neither mainstream American party likes to admit to this fact because of the implications for their respective political agendas, but in terms of concrete policy decisions Trump actually governed as a virulent Russia hawk who spent his entire term ramping up cold war aggressions against Russia on multiple fronts. He arguably played as much of a role in paving the way toward the war in Ukraine as any other president—it was Trump after all who first began pouring American weapons into Ukraine, an incendiary move that his predecessor Obama had actually resisted for fear of provoking Moscow.

The claim that Trump was a secret agent of the Kremlin has always been a ridiculous conspiracy theory made possible by mass-scale journalistic malpractice and intervention by the US intelligence cartel, and it has been debunked and discredited from pretty much every angle you could think of. But the strongest evidence that it was false was always the fact that Trump spent his entire presidency directly attacking Russian interests with actions like sanctions, shredded treaties, aggressive Nuclear Posture Reviews, efforts to shut down Nord Stream 2, occupying and repeatedly bombing Syria, and arming Ukraine.

Trump defenders will argue that Trump only did these things because he was politically pressured to by the Russiagate narrative, and that may be true, but what is the functional difference between a president who acts aggressively toward Russia because he was pressured to and a president who acts aggressively toward Russia because he wants to? In terms of actual behavior, there is no difference. If Trump is ramping up nuclear brinkmanship against Russia, it doesn't matter how his feelings secretly feel about it inside—all that matters is that it's happening. And if empire managers could pressure Trump to act as a Russia hawk before, there's no reason to believe they can't do it again.

The most significant thing about all US presidents is not their differences, it's their similarities. The truth of the matter is that if you were to only watch the movements of troops, war machinery, resources and money from year to year, you wouldn't be able to tell when one president's term ended and another began, or what party they belong to or what their campaign platform was. The empire marches on completely uninterrupted, regardless of who Americans elect to be the face at its front desk.

The bureaucracy is very strong, and it is that bureaucracy that rules the world.

Featured image via kremlin.ru (CC BY 4.0)

Rabbit Holes And Men Behind Curtains

You dive down rabbit hole after rabbit hole, searching for the man behind the curtain. You've seen enough to be convinced that everything you've been taught about the world is false, and now it's just a matter of finding out who's really responsible for making such a mess of things.

And for a while, your search seems fruitful. You discover that you don't really live in a democracy like you were taught where the public influences government behavior using their votes, or even in a separate sovereign nation like you learned in school. You discover that your country is part of a globe-spanning power structure which effectively functions as an empire—the most powerful empire ever to exist. And you discover that this empire has drivers who aren't beholden to the electorate in any meaningful way, acting not to advance the interests of the public but to advance the agenda of planetary domination.

So who are the drivers of the empire? You dive down more rabbit holes. You discover secretive government agencies with longtime operatives who don't leave with the outgoing official elected government, but stay on, helping to keep the gears of the empire turning regardless of who voters elect to be the face on the operation. You discover a revolving-door system in which the same empire managers are rotated in and out of positions in the official elected government, working in think tanks and military industrial complex advisory boards and mass media punditry when their party is out of office and rotating back in when their turn comes back around. You discover plutocrats who use their vast wealth to influence government policy via campaign donations, influential think tanks, mass media control and corporate lobbying, who often operate with—and profit from—a tremendous amount of overlap with government agencies. You discover organizations and institutions in which the wealthy and powerful congregate and coordinate to advance their agendas, often with a very high degree of secrecy.

But in all this rabbit holing and discovering, you still don't find any man behind the curtain. You come to see that any of the people you've been looking at could die tomorrow and the imperial machine would trudge on uninterrupted. There could be a giant violent revolution and these people could be guillotined by the thousands, and unless drastic changes were made to the systems which gave rise to them, someone else would just step in to fill their shoes.

So you start researching the systems. You start researching economic systems, financial systems, how resources are distributed, how money is allocated, how labor is exploited, how wealth is extracted. You come to see how our civilization has been turned into a giant wealth-generating machine for a class of wealthy exploiters using propaganda, property laws, artificial scarcity, enclosure of the commons and theft from indigenous populations, all wound around this made-up concept of money which translates directly into political power under our current systems. Because the people who are most adept at obtaining massive amounts of wealth/power are those who are sufficiently lacking in empathy to do whatever it takes to obtain it, we naturally find ourselves ruled by sociopaths. And we always will, until those systems change.

You dig even deeper. You discover that you haven't just been fed false information about how governments and nations work, you've been fed false information about even your most basic assumptions about reality. You discover in your own experience that there is no such thing as a separate self; that what we refer to linguistically as "I" and "me" are psychological delusions which underpin most of the suffering and dysfunctionality of the human species. In reality humans are inseparable from the biosphere from whence they emerged, which is in turn inseparable from the universe from whence it emerged, which is in turn inseparable from the Big-Bang-Or-Whatever-It-Was from whence it emerged. Everything is one, and the self is a lie.

And you realize that this is true of all the oligarchs and empire managers you've been staring at as well. They're not separate entities acting with agency in the world, they're clusters of conditioning and trauma which they inherited from their ancestors, which was passed down through their evolutionary heritage from the chaos and confusion inherent in existence as small prey animals who walked the earth millions of years ago. They're just swirling eddies in a sea of ineffable energy like anyone else, sleepwalking through life being whipped around by unconscious forces within themselves that they do not understand.

And you realize then that there is no man behind the curtain, and there never was. You ripped aside curtain after curtain hoping to find the man, and all you found was a man-shaped hole in the universe.

And you're not even mad. In fact, you find it hilarious. You laugh and you laugh at the silliness of it all. You laugh at how seriously we're all taking this game of separateness and enmity, and how seriously you'd been taking it just moments before. You laugh at how ultimately innocent we all are in all this, even the worst among us. You laugh at our cuteness. You laugh at this play of forms. And the universe laughs back. A laughing buddha, laughing at a universe made of laughing buddhas.

And you see, as you wipe the tears from your face, that everything is unfolding as it must. The universe is becoming more and more capable of perceiving itself—first with life, then with humans, then with the steady advancements in science and technology and psychology and awakening—and there's no reason to assume that this ongoing explosion of perception will stop. We're going to figure things out eventually. Consciousness keeps expanding. The light keeps getting brighter. The truth can only hide for so long.

Featured image via Creative Commons

Blinken: US Does Not Oppose Ukrainian Attacks Inside Russia With US–Supplied Missiles

During an appearance on ABC's This Week with Jonathan Karl, Secretary of State Tony Blinken explicitly said that the US would not oppose Ukraine using US-supplied longer-range missiles to attack deep inside Russian territory, a move that Moscow has previously called a "red line" which would make the United States a direct party to the conflict.

"We understand that the United States is considering sending those long-range missiles that Ukraine has been asking for for a long time," Karl said in the interview. "These are long-range missiles, 200 miles in range. Are you okay if those missiles allow Ukraine to attack deep into Russian territory?"

"In terms of their targeting decisions, it's their decision, not ours," answered Blinken after some bloviation.

"We've seen an increasing number of attacks on Russian territory by Ukrainian drones, some in Moscow, Rostov-on-Don just a couple of days ago. Did you bring that up?" asked Karl.

"No," said Blinken.

"Are you—are you okay with—I mean, obviously, they're—it's their decisions, but is this war now escalating into Russia?" asked Karl.

" Jon, we haven't encouraged and we haven't enabled any use of weapons outside of Ukraine's territory," Blinken said. "Having said that, let's take a step back for a second. Virtually every single day the Russians are attacking indiscriminately throughout the entire country of Ukraine. Just during the 48 hours that I was there going in, more missiles were launched at civilian targets, including in Kyiv while I was there; a horrific attack on a marketplace, people just going to buy food, civilians, had nothing to do with this war—killed 17 people. This is the daily life for Ukrainians. This is what they face every single day. So they have to make the basic decisions about how they're going to defend their territory and how they're working to take back what's been seized from them. Our role, the role of dozens of other countries around the world that are supporting them, is to help them do that. And ultimately, what we all want is an end to this Russian aggression and an end to the aggression that, again, is just and is durable. That's what Ukrainians want more than anyone else. That's what we're working toward."

The interview then concluded without any further follow-up from Karl. By successfully winding down the clock babbling about what Ukraine has a right to do, Blinken avoided discussing the real issue of what the US itself is doing. Nobody disputes that Ukraine has a right to attack Russian territory; Russia is attacking Ukrainian territory, so of course Ukraine has a right to retaliate. That is not being seriously debated anywhere. What's being debated is whether the US should be backing those attacks, because doing so could lead to nuclear war.

A year ago when Ukraine first started urging the United States to send it the Army Tactical Missile System (ATACMS)—which has nearly four times the range of the HIMARS weapons the US has been supplying—Russia's Foreign Ministry spokeswoman Maria Zakharova immediately responded with a warning that their use on Russian territory would make the US a direct participant in the conflict, and Russia would respond accordingly.

"If Washington decides to supply longer-range missiles to Kyiv, then it will be crossing a red line, and will become a direct party to the conflict," Zakharova said, adding that Russia "reserves the right to defend its territory."

As Michael Tracey noted on Twitter, Blinken was saying last year that Ukraine had provided assurances to the US that it would not use the other weapons systems the US has been supplying "against targets on Russian territory." Going by Blinken's current statements and the attacks we've been seeing from Ukraine inside the Russian Federation, this agreement appears no longer to be in place. Blinken has already previously voiced support for Ukrainian use of US-supplied weapons in Crimea, and now he's saying the US is fine with any US-supplied weapons being used on any Russian territory.

Which means there appears to have been yet another massive escalation between nuclear superpowers, which is once again going alarmingly under-reported by the western press.

In an article published in Antiwar this past July titled "ATACMS: Be Very Afraid of This Acronym," West Suburban Peace Coalition president Walt Zlotow wrote that this missile system "has potential to draw the US and NATO into all out war with Russia":

ATACMS are long range US missiles that can strike up to 190 miles. Top US officials, likely including President

Biden, are seriously considering giving ATACMS to Ukraine in their battle to take back all Russian gains in Ukraine, including Crimea. They can reach both Crimea and the Russian mainland.

If so used by Ukraine to attack Russia, it may be a missile too far that could ignite Russian tactical nuclear weapons in Ukraine. Further escalation into nuclear confrontation between Russia and the US/NATO alliance seeking Russia's defeat becomes more likely.

The US and its allies keep providing Ukraine with more and more offensive weapons that they had previously refused to supply for fear of getting drawn into the war and provoking a nuclear conflict. Last year Ukrainian Defense Minister Oleksii Reznikov correctly predicted that the US would wind up supplying the tanks, F-16s and ATACMS it had previously deemed too escalatory, because that had already been established as the trend from the beginning of the war.

"When I was in D.C. in November, before the invasion, and asked for Stingers, they told me it was impossible," Reznikov told The New Yorker last year. "Now it's possible. When I asked for 155-millimetre guns, the answer was no. HIMARS, no. HARM, no. Now all of that is a yes." He added, "Therefore, I'm certain that tomorrow there will be tanks and ATACMS and F-16s."

As Branko Marcetic explained earlier this year in an article for Responsible Statecraft titled "Mission Creep? How the US role in Ukraine has slowly escalated," this continual pattern of escalation is actually incentivizing Russia to start taking aggressive action against western powers so that its warnings and red lines will cease being ignored.

"By escalating their support for Ukraine's military, the U.S. and NATO have created an incentive structure for Moscow to take a drastic, aggressive step to show the seriousness of its own red lines," Marcetic writes. "This would be dangerous at the best of times, but particularly so when Russian officials are making clear they increasingly view the war as one against NATO as a whole, not merely Ukraine, while threatening nuclear response to the alliance's escalation in weapons deliveries."

"Moscow keeps saying escalatory arms transfers are unacceptable and could mean wider war; U.S. officials say since Moscow hasn't acted on those threats, they can freely escalate. Russia is effectively told it has to escalate to show it's serious about lines," Marcetic added on Twitter.

And it's just so strange how this isn't the main thing everyone talks about all the time. The fact that we are drawing closer and closer to nuclear conflict should dominate headlines every single day, and the subject of how to avoid planetary disaster should be the constant focus of mainstream political discourse. But it isn't, because that would interfere with the grand chessboard maneuverings of a globe-dominating empire working to secure unipolar planetary domination by undermining disobedient nations like Russia and China.

It's hard to think about the end of the world. It's hard to even wrap your mind around it, much less stand staring into the harsh white light of deep contemplation about what it is and what it would mean. A lot of cognitive dissonance and discomfort comes up, and it's easier to shift one's attention to something easier to chew on like the presidential race.

But this is something that urgently needs to be looked at. Because the people steering our world today appear to be driving blind.

•

Okinawa Disproves The US Narrative About Overseas Bases

Okinawa governor Denny Tamaki has implored the UN for international backing in his opposition to the prefecture being overrun with US military bases.

The Japan Times reports:

"I am here today to ask the world to witness the situation in Okinawa," Tamaki told a session of the world body's Human Rights Council, arguing that the concentration of the military bases there threatens peace.

Tamaki, the first Okinawa governor in eight years to address the council, said, "The reclamation work proceeds despite the fact that it was clearly opposed by Okinawan voters in a democratically held referendum."

Whenever I talk about the rapidly increasing number of US military bases and operations surrounding China I get empire simps telling me "But the people in those countries WANT us there!" Okinawa shows it's always been a nonconsensual relationship disguised as a consensual one.

And it should here be noted that Japan's national government was itself the product of extensive US manipulation after World War II. A 1994 New York Times article titled "C.I.A. Spent Millions to Support Japanese Right in 50's and 60's" details the massive amount of energy the US intelligence cartel poured into stomping down the Japan Socialist Party and ensuring that the Japanese right wing "maintained their one-party rule, forged close ties with Washington and fought off public opposition to the United States' maintaining military bases throughout Japan."

Featured image via Aaron on Flickr (CC BY-NC-SA 2.0)

If The US Really Was What It Pretends To Be

It's wild to consider how many of the world's problems would not exist if the US really was the thing it advertises itself as.

Ukraine would not be at war right now, because the US empire would not have provoked that war, since the US really would be an upholder of peace and international order.

The world would not be staring down the barrel of nuclear armageddon, because the US really would be a normal country that respects the sovereignty of other nations instead of the hub of a globe-spanning undeclared empire which keeps ramping up aggression against nuclear-armed states who refuse to consent to its planetary rule.

China would not be preparing for war, because the US military really would be used for the defense of the United States instead of rapidly encircling the US empire's top geopolitical rival with massive amounts of war machinery.

The middle east would not have spent the 21st century being ripped to pieces by western aggression, because the US really would care about the lives of the people who live there and not just pretend to in order to promote regime change interventionism.

Mountains of human corpses would not have been amassed in Yemen by violence, starvation and disease, because the US really would oppose tyrannical dictatorships like Saudi Arabia instead of enthusiastically facilitating their war crimes.

The information ecosystem of the western world would not be strangled by empire propaganda, internet censorship and Silicon Valley algorithm manipulation, because the US really would value free speech and free thought instead of churning out a continual barrage of mass-scale psychological operations designed to dominate the way people think, speak, work, act and vote.

Julian Assange would not be languishing in prison, because the US really would support press freedoms instead of working to set a legal precedent normalizing the persecution of journalists for reporting inconvenient facts.

The people of the United States would not be floundering in poverty and broken infrastructure, because they really would live in a democracy that allows them to influence government policy instead of an oligarchy rigged to benefit the rich and powerful at the expense of normal human beings.

The US would not be a tyrannical police state with the largest incarceration rate on the planet, because the US government really would care about civil rights and liberty instead of only caring about the profits that can be harvested via prison slavery and private prisons from those citizens who don't make good cogs in the capitalist machine.

Developing nations would be thriving a lot more, because the US really would support their national sovereignty and independence instead of doing whatever's necessary to facilitate the imperialist extraction of their wealth.

Human civilization would be far more just and equitable than it currently is, because the US really would value every nation's right to forge its own path, and therefore would not have spent generations aggressively stomping out every attempt to move toward socialism everywhere in the world.

The planet would not be circled by hundreds of foreign US military bases and continually terrorized by US wars of aggression, proxy conflicts, CIA coups and starvation sanctions, because all the US government secrecy which makes this malfeasance possible wouldn't

exist, since the US really would value truth and transparency instead of power and domination.

The world would be a much more healthy and harmonious place if the US really was the peace-loving, tyranny-opposing democracy that it and all its propaganda systems frame it as. But because the US government is actually the most tyrannical regime on earth and values nothing apart from its own ability to dominate as many members of the human species as possible, we live in a world of far greater peril and abuse than we otherwise would.

I write so much about the US empire because that's just what you find yourself doing when you set out to describe the problems of our world with an open mind; trace those problems back to their origins, and many of them revolve around this strange and profoundly abusive power structure which manages to evade much criticism and scrutiny because it has the most sophisticated soft power narrative control systems ever devised.

The US empire depends on keeping the world asleep to its abusiveness. And the world depends on everyone waking up to it.

Featured image via Adobe Stock

Queen Warmonger Hillary Clinton Complains About "Men Starting Wars"

Some days the Caitlin Johnstone articles just write themselves.

During her self-titled annual awards ceremony at Georgetown University on Thursday, Hillary Clinton said that the biggest obstacle to peace and security around the world is "men starting wars."

During the Q&A segment of the event, Clinton was asked by a student, "What do you see as the biggest challenge for women, peace, and security over the next ten years?"

"Well I think the biggest challenge is men starting wars," Clinton replied, adding, "You know, I don't think they have enough to do."

Which would have come across as a humorous and relatable answer, if it had come from pretty much anyone else on the entire planet.

The single strongest argument against Hillary Rodham Clinton's suggestion that only men start wars is the career of Hillary Rodham Clinton. This is after all the same woman who chortled with delight when she found out Muammar Gaddafi had been lynched in the streets following his US-led overthrow in Libya during her tenure as secretary of state, saying "I'm sure it did" when asked if his death had anything to do with her visit to the country. The same woman who as secretary of state promoted the plan of arming extremists in Syria with the goal of toppling Damascus. The same woman who as a senator played a pivotal role in convincing the Democratic Party to support the invasion of Iraq based on lies. The same woman who as first lady said she "urged" her husband Bill Clinton to launch the bombing campaign that would leave Serbia and Kosovo covered in cluster munitions. The same woman who as a US presidential candidate advocated a no-fly zone in Syria which would have required attacks on Russian war planes who violated it, and endorsed the same brinkmanship policies in Ukraine which eventually provoked the Russian invasion.

When Tulsi Gabbard famously dubbed Clinton "the queen of warmongers" in 2019, it wasn't just empty rhetoric. There is no woman alive who anyone could argue is more deserving of that title. If you'd have told me there was a Hillary Rodham Clinton Awards ceremony prior to my having read about it, I would have assumed it was an event where women receive trophies for killing large numbers of human beings with military violence.

It is of course true that men have been the drivers of the overwhelming majority of wars throughout the ages, but that's just what's so disgusting about the modern iteration of "feminism" that Hillary Clinton rode to prominence on. The girlboss "feminism" of the Hillary Clinton age has ceased to mean advancing women's interests and ensuring that women are treated as equals to men, and has become a vapid celebration of examples of women proving that they can be just as murderous, tyrannical and abusive as any man.

That was the zeitgeist that Hillary Clinton rode her 2016 presidential campaign on, and when the American public recoiled in horror and refused to vote for her, it was spun as a victory for misogyny. It should have been spun as a victory for would-be bombing victims who live in US-targeted nations.

Hillary Clinton is all the worst things about modern liberals and the Democratic Party. She is a blood-spattered psychopath who has dedicated her life to serving all the worst impulses of the human species—imperialism, militarism, capitalism, authoritarianism, and, yes, patriarchy—wearing a grinning plastic mask of civil rights and social justice to convince people to let her in the door.

She's one of the creepiest things you could possibly imagine, and the sooner her and those like her are gone and forgotten, the better.

•

The News Has Nothing To Do With Newsworthiness

I don't mention it often but I actually have a degree in journalism. I graduated with distinction from the Royal Melbourne Institute of Technology in 2003, and while it would be another 13 years before I'd ever put my degree to any use, the experience played a massive role in forming my opinions about the mainstream press.

One of the lessons I think about a lot came at the beginning of my two-week internship with Channel 10's Eyewitness News (now 10 News First) when I was watching the show's bedraggled news editor put everyone's story assignments up on the whiteboard one morning. I'd been paying a lot of attention to TV news at the time because that's what we were studying, and I'd noticed that the stories Channel 10 would cover were always exactly the same as the ones that would be covered by Channel 7 and Channel 9— usually in exactly the same order.

"Why do you guys always cover the same stories as Channel 7 and Channel 9?" I asked. "Do you guys phone each other to coordinate?"

He laughed.

"No, but it is a bit strange isn't it?" he agreed. "I guess it's what you call 'news sense'."

Even back then I had a hard time believing that all news editors had some magical "sense" which caused them each to know which are the most newsworthy stories day after day in a whole world full of events and ordeals.

Since that time I've learned about the groupthink effect that working in the mainstream press tends to have on people's minds according to those who've made careers there, and the fact that journalists who either don't know how to or don't care to dance to the the agenda-setting task of the plutocratic media don't find themselves promoted to news editor. It's not that editors are coordinating with each other across outlets or receiving instructions on what to report from oligarchs and government agencies, it's that if they were the type who needed to do such things to know what to report, they wouldn't be working where they're working.

How did the mainstream press know to ignore the scandal of a Ukrainian Nazi being applauded in the Canadian parliament? How did they know to smear Bernie Sanders and Jeremy Corbyn? How do they know to support every war while ignoring homelessness and economic injustice? It sure ain't "news sense".

In a contentious 1996 discussion between Noam Chomsky and British journalist Andrew Marr, Chomsky described a "filtering system" that "selects for obedience and subordination" which determines who gets to the top of the most influential platforms in the western world. He derided the false image that mainstream journalists have of themselves as "a crusading profession" who are "adversarial" and "stand up against power," saying it's almost impossible for a good journalist to do so in any meaningful way in the western press.

"How can you know that I'm self-censoring?" Marr objected. "How can you know that journalists are—"

"I'm not saying you're self-censoring," Chomsky replied. "I'm sure you believe everything you're saying. But what I'm saying is that if you believed something different, you wouldn't be sitting where you're sitting."

In a 1997 essay, Chomsky added that "the point is that they wouldn't be there unless they had already demonstrated that nobody has to tell them what to write because they are going to say the right thing anyway."

By the time I graduated I'd already figured out that I wouldn't be able to use my journalism degree to do any actual journalism. It had been made abundantly clear to me that I'd have to spend my first years re-writing copy from Reuters and AP and avoiding making any waves, and that even if I made it past that point there was very little to look forward to; the TV reporters at Channel 10 would write their stories before going to the scene of their reporting and just look for things that support their pre-written narrative, so there was never any actual fact-finding or real journalism happening on the ground.

So I didn't bother. I raised some kids, did some corporate work, ran a business and a little eco-blog, and spend time learning about life instead. I couldn't have predicted that the internet would eventually give rise to a new wave of crowdfunded journalism which would make it possible for me to spend my time on this planet doing what I do today. But now that it has I find myself thinking back on that news editor at Eyewitness News, and noticing that the stories I focus on are almost never the same ones being covered by the mainstream press on any given day.

Image by Adobe Stock

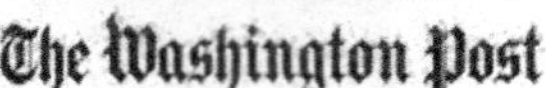

The Washington Post
Democracy Dies in Darkness

WAR IN UKRAINE   Live briefing   Verified videos   Donbas region   Russian combat capabilities   HIMAR

Opinion | Ukraine aid is a great investment. Don't let MAGA Republicans end it.

By Max Boot
Columnist | + Follow

This Proxy War Can't Be Both 'Unprovoked' AND A Great Strategic Investment

As opposition to funding the US proxy war in Ukraine increases on Capitol Hill, empire apologists have been frantically churning out think pieces about how much the war serves US strategic interests in order to manufacture support for its continued backing by Washington. Such arguments flatly contradict the propaganda messaging we were inundated with at the beginning of the war that this was an "unprovoked invasion", but empire managers don't seem particularly interested in defending that narrative anymore.

The latest appearance in this new "our Ukraine proxy warfare greatly advances US strategic interests" genre of op-ed comes to us courtesy of notorious war propagandist Max Boot via The Washington Post. Boot's article was originally titled "Ukraine aid is a great investment. Don't let MAGA Republicans end it.", but the headline has since been revised to the slightly less creepy "This is what the U.S. is getting by aiding Ukraine."

Claiming that funding the war is "the right thing to do strategically," Boot argues that "it is hard to think of any U.S. foreign policy initiative since the end of the Cold War that has been more successful or more important than U.S. aid to Ukraine."

"Russia has lost an estimated 120,000 soldiers and 170,000 to 180,000 have been injured," Boot writes. "Russia has also lost an estimated 2,329 tanks, 2,817 infantry fighting vehicles, 2,868 trucks and jeeps, 354 armored personnel carriers, 538 self-propelled artillery vehicles, 310 towed artillery pieces, 92 fixed-wing aircraft and 106 helicopters."

"The Russian armed forces have been devastated, thereby reducing the risk to front-line NATO states such as Poland and the Baltic republics that the United States is treaty-bound to protect," Boot continues. "And all of that has been accomplished without having to put a single U.S. soldier at risk on the front lines."

"That's an incredible investment," gloats Boot.

At no time in his masturbatory gushing about how many Russians this war has helped kill does Boot make any mention of the immense toll this deliberately provoked and completely unnecessary war has taken on Ukrainian lives. Their deaths and dismemberments and displacement are the largest price being paid into this "investment" by far, but Boot doesn't deem them worthy of even a footnote.

We've been seeing this "investment" line being promoted with increasing frequency by US empire managers and their apologists. In an article published in the Connecticut Post last month, Senator Richard Blumenthal assured Americans that "we're getting our money's worth on our Ukraine investment." A few days prior to that Senator Mitt Romney had described the proxy war as "the best national defense spending I think we've ever done," because "We're diminishing and devastating the Russian military for a very small amount of money… a weakened Russia is a good thing." In December Senate Minority Leader Mitch McConnell said that funding the proxy war is "a direct investment in reducing Vladimir Putin's future capabilities to menace America, threaten our allies and contest our core interests." Last November the imperial war machine-funded think tank Center for European Policy Analysis published a report arguing that "US spending of 5.6% of its defense budget to destroy nearly half of Russia's conventional military capability seems like an absolutely incredible investment."

We saw one of the most glaring examples of this new genre of empire apologia last week, when the Bill Kristol-led group "Republicans for Ukraine" put out a television ad explaining how much this war is a fantastic investment which serves US strategic interests.

"When America arms Ukraine, we get a lot for a little," the ad said. "Putin is an enemy of America. We've used 5% of our defense budget to arm Ukraine, and with it, they've destroyed 50% of Putin's Army. We've done all this by sending weapons from storage, not our troops. The more Ukraine weakens Russia, the more it also weakens Russia's closest ally, China."

We are asked to believe a lot of very stupid things by the propagandists of the US-centralized empire, but one of the very stupidest is the claim that this war simultaneously (A) was completely unprovoked, and (B) just coincidentally happens to massively advance US strategic interests.

It really cannot be both. If you accept that this war is a very low-cost, high-reward means for the US to advance its strategic interests overseas, then you'd have to have tapioca for brains to also believe that the US wouldn't have gone out of its way to make sure the war happens. And indeed that's exactly what occurred, which is why US intelligence operatives and western foreign policy analysts spent years saying that the actions of the US and its allies were going to provoke Russia to war.

The reason it matters so much that the war in Ukraine was provoked by the US-centralized empire is because that shows you where the path to peace lies. When empire simps object to criticisms of western proxy warfare in Ukraine with "Oh so you're saying we should just ABANDON THE UKRAINIANS and let Putin take over the country???", what they are missing is that this is not a war between only Russia and Ukraine, and

Russia doesn't see it as such. Russia believes it is fighting a war against the aggression and expansionism of the NATO alliance, which the head of NATO himself recently confirmed. What this means is that the NATO alliance can facilitate peace in Ukraine by agreeing to roll back the aggressions which led to this war in the first place.

NATO powers have always been fully aware that they could bring about peace in Ukraine in this way, but they choose not to move NATO war machinery away from Russia's borders and grant Moscow the same freedom from military threats in its immediate surroundings that Washington insists on in its own immediate surroundings. The managers of the empire chose not to do this, and indeed actually sabotaged peace negotiations in the early days of the conflict, because they firmly believe that this war advances their interests.

This is what empire apologists are omitting from the story when they claim that Putin can end this war by withdrawing troops from Ukraine; they are leaving out their own government's role in starting and perpetuating this war. To demand that Russia cease its aggressions, without the western empire ceasing the aggressions which provoked the war in the first place, is to demand that Russia lie down and submit itself to the dictates of the empire. People who call for an end to Russian aggressions but not the western aggressions Russia is reacting to don't really want peace, they just want the empire to conquer and subjugate the insolent curs who dared to defy it.

It's good to be clear on this, because it shows who the obstacles to peace really are. The longer we pretend the only people keeping this war going reside in Moscow, the longer any path toward peace will elude us.

•

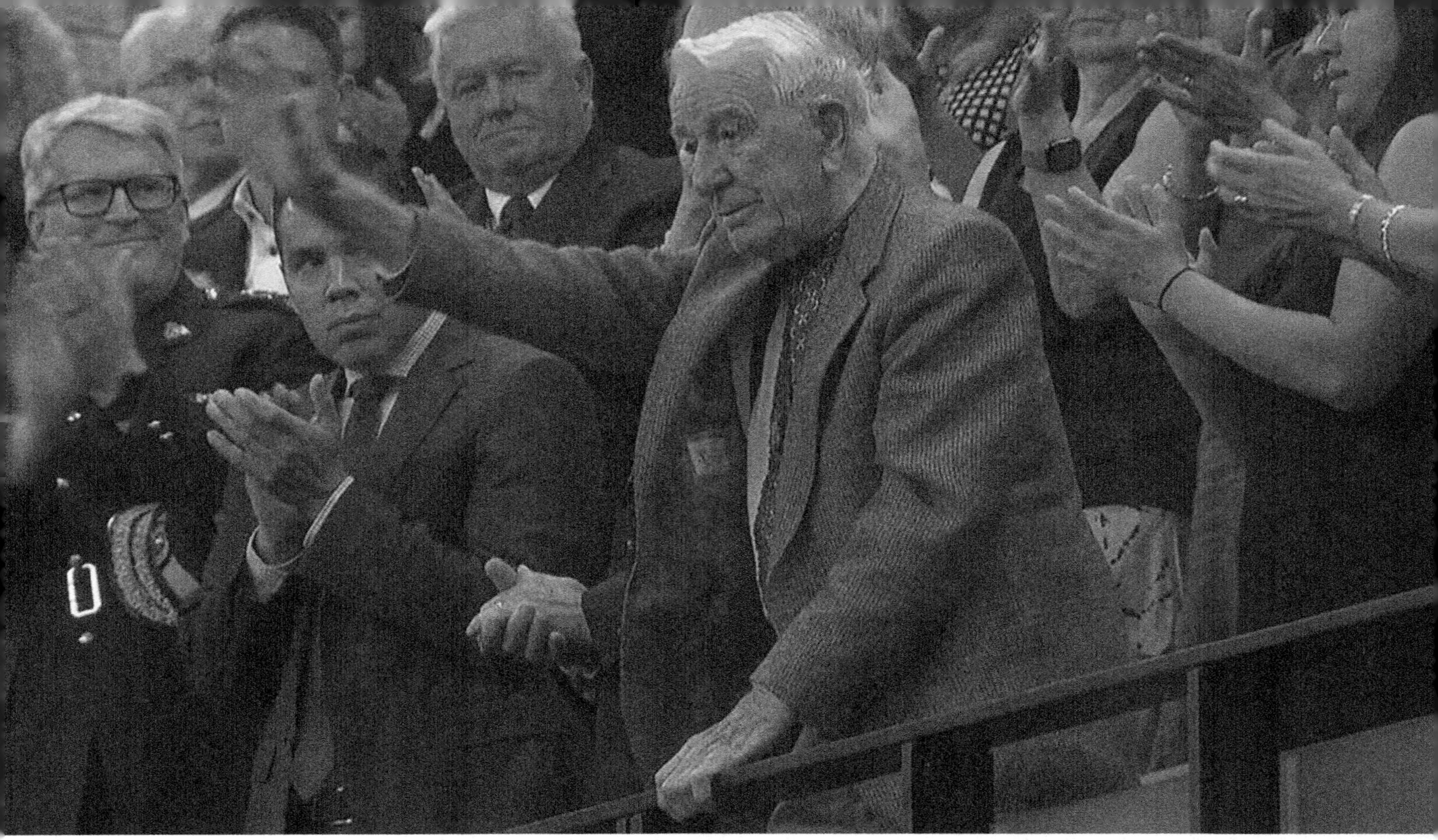

Nobody Who Fought Against Russia Could Possibly Be Bad!

Just because Ukraine has Nazi paramilitaries and just because it's impossible to take photos of Ukrainian soldiers without capturing Nazi insignia and just because Ukrainian Nazis get applauded in parliament doesn't mean we're on the side of the Nazis, you crazy Russian shill.

Caitlin Johnstone
@caitoz

This is like calling Ringo Starr a "Beatles-linked musician". He was part of the band, mate.

POLITICO @politico · Sep 25
Nazi-linked veteran received ovation during Zelenskyy's Canada visit
politico.com/news/2023/09/2....

Rate proposed Community Notes

11:20 AM · Sep 25, 2023 · **411.1K** Views

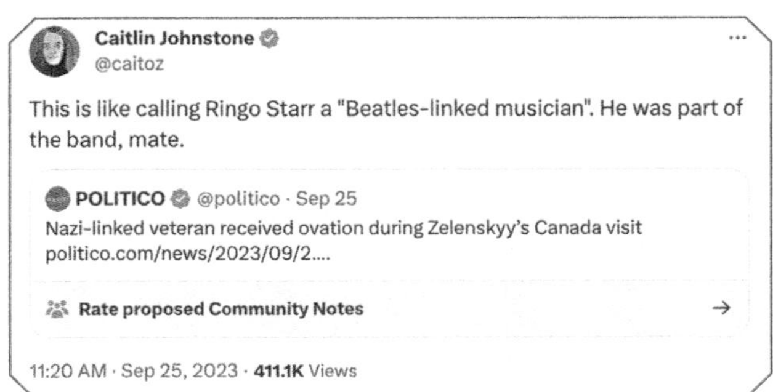

Western minds have become so warped by cold war hysteria these last few years that it never occurred to a single person in an entire giant room full of professional politicians that someone who fought against Russia during World War II might be a bad guy. Having fought against Russia at any point in history is just reflexively assumed to have put you on the right side.

In Support Of The Policy Of Deterrence

There's been a lot of debate lately over the US strategy of surrounding nations like Russia and China with war machinery in order to deter them from aggressive actions. Some argue that since powerful nations tend to respond aggressively to the amassing of military threats on their borders, this policy actually provokes the very aggressions its proponents claim it prevents.

And to these people I say: hogwash. Only peaceful and harmonious responses can possibly be expected from policies of military encirclement.

That's why I propose that the People's Liberation Army should begin militarily encircling the continental United States with Chinese war machinery as quickly as possible, in order to deter future US aggression around the world.

The US has after all been the single most aggressive government on the world stage for generations now. It has repeatedly invaded and staged regime change operations against its neighbors in Latin America, to say nothing of its military aggressions and proxy warfare in nations like Vietnam, Laos, Cambodia, Iraq, Afghanistan, Libya, Syria and Yemen. No other government has spent the 21st century killing people by the millions in wars of aggression. No other government has been surrounding the planet with hundreds of military bases, deliberately targeting civilian populations with deadly force around the world via starvation sanctions, and working continuously to topple any government on earth which disobeys its dictates. Only the US has.

Therefore as a Super Serious Foreign Policy Pundit I recommend that China begin working with the leftist governments in Latin America which have a contentious relationship with Washington and establishing some military alliances of mutual defense, ideally including Russia and Iran in those alliances as well.

Hopefully Mexico will allow China to construct missile systems and military bases along the US border, and the Chinese navy can continually patrol US coastlines to ensure that its aggressions remain fully contained.

Some of the people with whom I've shared this proposal objected that it would instantly provoke a war and result in a great increase in the military violence I aim to deter, including increasing the likelihood of nuclear war. So naturally I screamed at those people and called them appeasers and White House propagandists.

"You're basically another Neville Chamberlain!" I shrieked. "If it had been up to you we'd have appeased Hitler and made deals with Nazi Germany! You American troll! You Biden puppet!"

These people just don't understand how deterrence works. If history has shown us anything, it's that amassing military threats on the borders of powerful nations only ever leads to peace and love, and has never caused anything bad to happen at any time ever.

I am a very reasonable person. Everyone should listen to me. Give me a big house and a senior fellowship at an influential think tank.

·

Modern Empire Apologia Is Mostly Just Westerners Arguing With Reality

It's funny how much empire apologia in the 2020s consists of westerners saying that governments who aren't aligned with the United States shouldn't have the security concerns they have and shouldn't regard their national interests the way they do.

Armchair proxy warriors against Russia defend the NATO expansionism which led to the war in Ukraine by saying that Russia should simply not have taken issue with a western military alliance amassing war machinery on its doorstep. If you bring up the fact that a great many western analysts spent a great many years warning that the actions of NATO powers after the fall of the USSR was going to provoke Russia into war, their only argument is to say that Russia should not have been provoked by those actions.

You see the same thing with regard to China. Beijing's standoff with Taiwan is essentially an unresolved civil war that's been frozen in its current state (largely by US interventionism) since the creation of the PRC, with a historical background that stretches back centuries. The western response to the Chinese push to reunify the island with the mainland has been to insist that Beijing simply begin regarding Taiwan as a sovereign nation, despite the fact that those western governments themselves do not recognize Taiwan's sovereignty due to the complex nature of the standoff.

In both cases, the US-centralized empire is confronting nations which have policies and positions in place regarding their immediate surroundings which run much deeper and go much further back than vapid liberal idealism. Russia was invaded through Ukraine by both Napoleon and Hitler. Taiwan was used by the Japanese as an unsinkable aircraft carrier from which to continuously attack the Chinese mainland during World War Two. You can disagree with the deep-rooted security concerns of these nations if you want, but what you can't do is simply hand-wave them away just because they don't fit in with the made-up rules the west likes to pretend it plays by.

The reason foreign policy realists like John Mearsheimer were able to correctly predict years in advance that the west's aggressions toward Russia meant that "Ukraine is going to get wrecked" was because they were just looking objectively at the raw data of what the west was doing and what Russia's national security positions were. They weren't fixating on ideological shoulds and shouldn'ts or babbling about what would be the just and moral position for Russia to have in some alternate hypothetical universe, they were focused on what was happening and what would happen. And a lot of death and destruction would have been avoided if they'd been listened to.

Instead, the empire has opted to barrel forward with its aggressions against Russia and is now doing the same with China, and anyone who points out that these are terrifyingly incendiary provocations gets shouted down by what essentially amount to arguments against reality.

That's the main tool in the empire apologist's toolbox these days: arguing with reality. If you point out the reality of where people are at in Moscow and Beijing with regard to western provocations on their nations' borders, their only answer is to say "Yeah well that's not how things should be so we're going to keep doing what we're doing."

It's like being warned that you'll get punched if you keep yelling ethnic slurs in public but doing it anyway because you believe people should respect free speech, and then melodramatically clutching your broken nose and yelling that what happened should not have happened. Reality doesn't care about your ideological shoulds and shouldn'ts; as far as reality is concerned, there's just what happens and what does not happen. If you actually want to avoid certain outcomes, you can't just heap a bunch of conceptual shoulds and shouldn't on concrete circumstances—you've got to actually conduct yourself in a way that steers clear of those outcomes.

And the issue here is of course that the western empire doesn't really want to avoid those outcomes. It stood everything to gain by provoking the war in Ukraine, and preventing the rise of China by any means necessary is an absolutely fundamental requirement for securing US planetary hegemony. The empire is just doing what it wants to do regardless of the consequences, and its propaganda machine is churning out shoulds and shouldn'ts in order to justify those actions that trusting members of the public then go on to regurgitate.

Arguing with reality never works, whether you're talking about international relations, interpersonal relationships, or the inner workings of your own mind. The way out of suffering is the same on any scale: dealing with reality as it actually is, and working with life on life's terms.

Image via Adobe Stock

People Are Dying For Inches In Ukraine, The "World's Largest Arms Fair"

There's a heartbreaking graphic going around right now showing the almost microscopic changes that have occurred to the frontline of the war in Ukraine this year despite nonstop death and destruction of unfathomable horror the entire time.

The graphic comes from a New York Times article titled "Who's Gaining Ground in Ukraine? This Year, No One.", which eventually gets around to acknowledging that Russia has actually gained more ground than Ukraine in 2023 despite Kyiv's much-hyped counteroffensive which began in June.

"When both sides' gains are added up, Russia now controls nearly 200 square miles more territory in Ukraine compared with the start of the year," the Times reports.

As Left I on the News noted on Twitter, this contradicts the titular claim in another New York Times article published last week under the headline "Ukraine Has Gained Ground. But It Has Much Further To Go."

The reason the map of gains and losses is so heartbreaking is because so much has been given up for so very, very little. At least tens of thousands have died in this war with hundreds of thousands wounded, all for those teeny, tiny little blips on the map. Ukraine is now freckled with more landmines than anywhere else on earth, which experts say will take decades to clear. This giant deathtrap is exacerbated by the cluster munitions that are covering the land with greater and greater frequency, which will go on to detonate and kill civilians (mostly children) for years to come. The mines and artillery fire on the frontline of this war are reportedly creating tens of thousands of amputees, numbers comparable to what was seen in World War I.

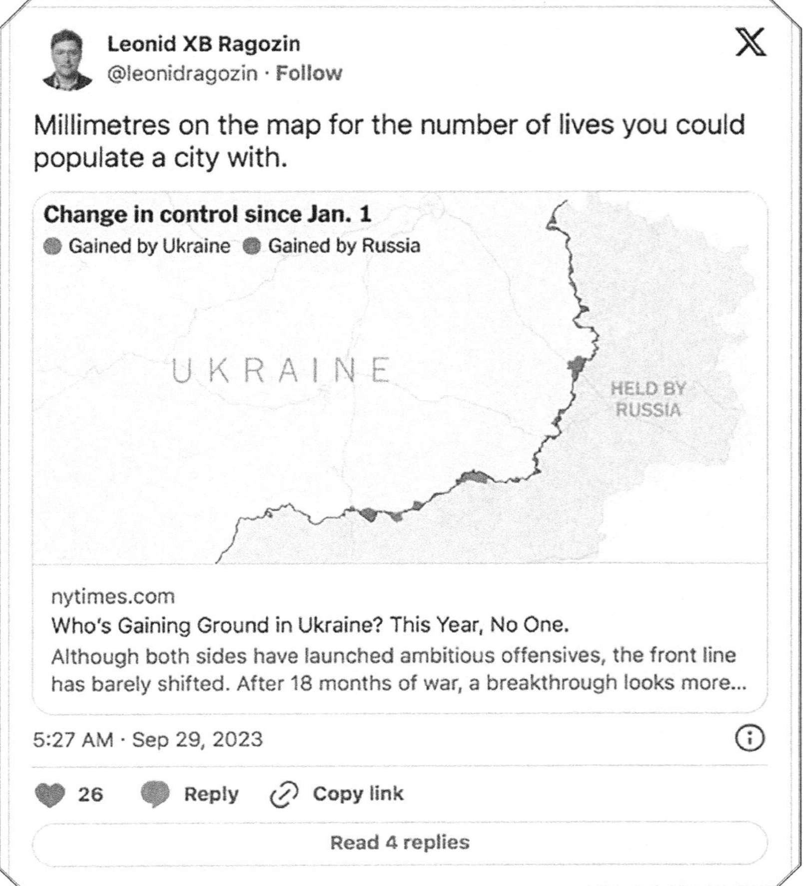

And all for what? Essentially nothing. A few inches gained here, a few inches lost there. The meaninglessness of it all is probably one of the reasons why military-aged Ukrainian men have been fleeing and attempting to flee the nation in droves to avoid conscription.

War is the worst thing in the world. The suffering, trauma and loss of mass military violence is too much to comprehend, even for people who are right there experiencing it. And the only thing worse than a war where one side gets completely steamrolled by the other is one in which people keep killing each other and killing each other over tiny gains and losses on the battlefield without an end to the nightmare anywhere on the horizon.

And now we see western officials and media outlets telling us all to prepare for this war to drag on for years, potentially into the 2030s. This nonsensical violence, which even the head of NATO now admits could have been avoided by simply ceasing to amass a western military threat on Russia's doorstep, is scheduled to drag on as long as possible for no grander reason than the advancement of US strategic interests.

This news from The New York Times comes out at the same time as a Wall Street Journal article titled "The War in Ukraine Is Also a Giant Arms Fair," subtitled "Arms makers are getting orders for weapons being put to the test on the battlefield."

"The Panzerhaubitze howitzer is part of an arsenal of weapons being put to the test in Ukraine in what has become the world's largest arms fair," writes WSJ's Alistair MacDonald. "Companies that make the weapons being used in Ukraine have won orders and resurrected production lines. The deployment of billions of dollars worth of equipment in a major land war has also given manufacturers and militaries a unique opportunity to analyze the battlefield performance of weapons, and learn how best to use them."

This is one of those things that just sounds a bit uncomfortable at first, but if you really sit with the words and deeply contemplate what's being said here it will show up as so deeply evil it will give you nightmares. The fact that weapons systems are being tested on human bodies to the immense benefit of war profiteers over a completely avoidable and deliberately provoked war is one of the most depraved things you can possibly imagine, and is a clear sign that we are living in a profoundly sick society.

This is so, so ugly, and it's slated to get even uglier—these freaks haven't even gotten started on China yet. The sooner this monstrous power structure can be brought to its knees, the better it will be for everyone.

·

Unprecedented Times Call For Unprecedented Measures

Whenever I talk about the kinds of changes human civilization is going to have to make if we want our species to survive into the future, I always get people saying that no such civilization has ever existed in all of human history. That at no time has there ever been a large industrialized civilization wherein human behavior was driven by collaboration rather than competition; wherein the profit motive was eliminated as a driver of civilization; wherein humans work in cooperation with the ecosystem for the good of all beings; wherein peace and harmony prevail and everyone has enough.

And of course, they are correct. At no time has any civilization like that ever existed. But at no time has humanity ever been in the situation it's in currently, either.

At no other time in history have humans been so close to destroying the biosphere with their profit-driven behavior. At no time have there ever been this many humans on this planet. At no time have there ever been billions of human brains networked with each other in real time the way ours are now via the internet.

That last one's kind of a big deal, by the way. The fact that billions of human beings now have access to (A) all the information known to man and (B) instantaneous communication with each other is far and away the most significant thing ever to happen to our species since the evolution of the human brain, and it will get even more significant as improved translation services network us even further. Though from the outside we might look more or less the same way we looked three decades ago, in reality there have probably been more significant changes in our species in the last three decades than in the previous three millennia. Humans are functionally a very, very different kind of organism than they were before you and I were born.

We have literally never been here before. We've never seen anything remotely like this. Not even close. We are in completely uncharted territory.

These are wildly unprecedented times, and unprecedented times call for unprecedented measures. Because our situation is so dramatically unlike anything we've ever seen before, the same must also necessarily be true of the solutions to the problems we now face. If there's a way out of this mess, it's going to look unlike anything we've ever seen before.

Our species is at an adaptation-or-extinction juncture at this point in spacetime. We're staring down the barrel of total extinction via nuclear armageddon or environmental collapse. Everything that got us to this point is the result of the behavior patterns we've been moving in for the centuries leading up to it.

Listen to the MUSTN'TS, child,
Listen to the DON'TS
Listen to the SHOULDN'TS
The IMPOSSIBLES, the WONT'S
Listen to the NEVER HAVES
Then listen close to me—
Anything can happen, child,
ANYTHING can be.

~ Shel Silverstein

What this means is that any deviation away from our trajectory toward annihilation will necessarily entail a drastic unpatterning, since you cannot separate our circumstances from the patterns which gave rise to it. Even if you could wave a magic wand and have our biosphere perfectly healthy again and all nuclear weapons reduced to atoms, our behavior patterns would just cause us to destroy the biosphere again and rebuild the nukes in a matter of years.

So if we are to survive into the future, we're going to have to drastically change our patterns. We're going to have to begin acting in ways we have never acted before so that we can begin organizing civilization in a way that it has never before existed.

So sure, maybe I am being unrealistic in describing the radically divergent kind of civilization we're going to have to create... but it's also the only kind of future civilization that can possibly exist. If it's impossible to create a wildly different kind of civilization than the kind we've been living in, then it's also impossible that humans exist in future centuries, because we will necessarily wipe ourselves out with our self-destructive patternings otherwise.

So while I am talking about a future civilization that sounds utopian, I am also talking about the only kind of future civilization that can possibly exist. If there are future generations, they will necessarily be living in a society that functions in a completely different way than our current one does.

And I personally believe it's possible. I really think we can make the adaptation-or-extinction jump if we want to. In wildly unprecedented times, no possibility is off the table.

Image via Adobe Stock

Reflections (On A Prison Bus)
Caitlin Johnstone
16" x 20", oil on canvas

Journalism Itself Is Locked Up In Belmarsh

As the 17th anniversary of the creation of WikiLeaks passes us by, it's probably worth taking a moment to reflect on Julian Assange and what his persecution means for us and our society.

Because in a very real sense, it's not just a man locked up in Belmarsh Prison for the crime of good journalism—it's journalism itself. It's the idea that anyone should be permitted to expose the criminality of the world's most powerful and tyrannical people. It's the idea that the public should be allowed to know what abuses the US empire is committing around the world.

Julian Assange is the world's greatest journalist. By revolutionizing source protection for the digital age with the creation of WikiLeaks 17 years ago and then going on to break some of the biggest stories of the 21st century, Assange set himself head and shoulders above any other living reporter anywhere on earth. And by showing the world that they can lock up the world's greatest journalist for revealing inconvenient truths, they are showing the world that they can lock up anyone.

That's what this case has always been about. It's not about whether Assange crossed some arbitrary procedural line when working with Chelsea Manning to expose US war crimes. It's not about the US protecting its national security. It's not about any of the other justifications people have put forward to excuse their sycophantic support for the persecution of a journalist for doing journalism. It's about setting a legal precedent that will allow the US empire to extradite anyone anywhere in the world who reveals inconvenient facts about it. It's about showing all journalists everywhere that if they can do it to the greatest among them, they can do it to any of them. And, like so much else in the world today, it's about narrative control.

To accept the persecution of Julian Assange is to accept the idea that all media everywhere must function as propaganda organs of the US government. It's to take it as a given that any journalist anywhere in the world who decides to do real journalism and expose inconvenient facts about the powerful in the public interest should be jailed until they can be extradited to the United States for a show trial, and then left to rot in one of the most draconian prison systems on the planet. It's to accept that we will never live in a truth-based society guided by facts and information, and must forever resign ourselves to living in a society dominated by the whims of the powerful.

Your position on the Assange case is therefore your position on what kind of society we should hope to live in, and what kind of future we should hope to have. In a very real way, it's your position on humanity itself.

Should humanity try to create a better world, or should we keep plunging into dystopia until we are driven into nuclear war or environmental catastrophe by rulers we are forbidden to question? Do we want to move into the light, or into the darkness? Your position on Assange shows your answer to these questions, and shows which course you want us to take.

•

At London arms fair, global war fears are good for business

By **Peter Apps**

September 15, 2023 7:53 PM GMT+10 · Updated 4 days ago

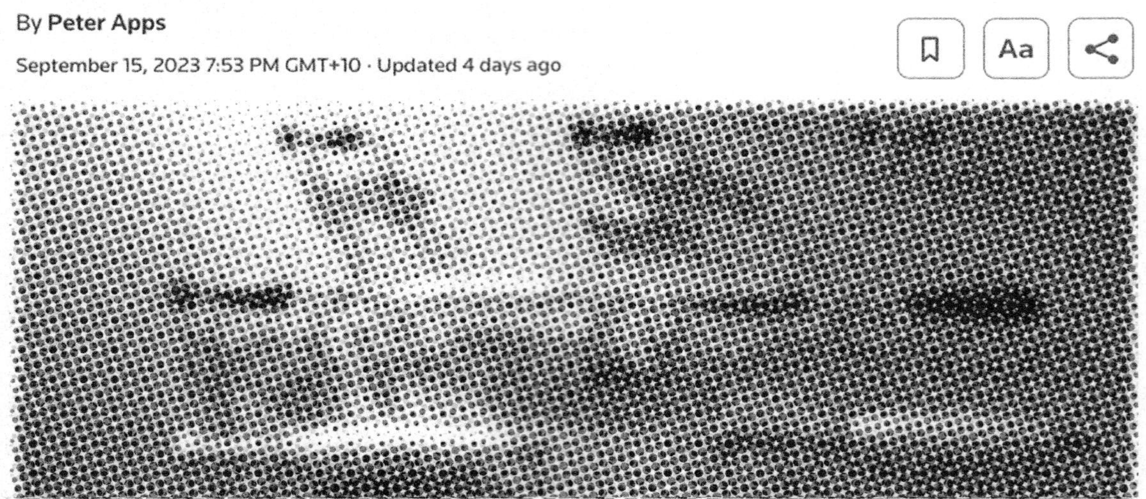

War Profiteers Are A Sign Of A Profoundly Sick Society

"War is good for business."

So reads a quote from an arms industry executive in a recent Reuters article titled "At London arms fair, global war fears are good for business" about Europe's biggest arms show, the biennial Defence and Security Equipment International. You will probably be unsurprised to learn that Reuters does not name the war profiteer whose quote inspired their headline.

The article describes the way the war in Ukraine and brinkmanship in Taiwan is leading to surging profits for the military industrial complex, with the UK doubling its arms exports in 2022 and worldwide military spending expected to continue to rise by four percent each year for the next five years. According to the Stockholm International Peace Research Institute, European military spending rose 13 percent in 2022 alone, bringing total global spending to an all-time high of $2.24 trillion.

"We are extremely busy," an exaltant head of sales at an armored steel company tells Reuters.

War is good for business, and it's expected to get even better. The world's largest military contractor Lockheed Martin saw its stock rise by a whopping 37 percent last year—helped along by taxpayer-sponsored stock buybacks—and in a report titled "Lockheed Martin: Huge Growth Ahead", an investment analyst for AlmaStreet Capital predicted last month that Lockheed's massive profits will only continue to climb. Calling the escalated geopolitical tensions in the current political atmosphere "the most favorable condition that Lockheed Martin could possibly operate under," the article's author writes the following:

"Governments worldwide are increasing their budget for defense and security under this heightened geopolitical tensions worldwide. The US government is not an exception. As the largest contractor to the US government, Lockheed Martin is bound to be the biggest beneficiary of the increased defense budget. Given that the company already reached approximately 8% of YoY net sales growth in 2Q23, I believe escalating geopolitical tensions along with easing macroeconomic conditions would allow Lockheed Martin to soon achieve double-digit growth in net sales by the end of the year."

So it's no wonder that Lockheed CEO James Taiclet called the most recent hike in the US military budget "as good an outcome as our industry or our company could ask for." There are vast fortunes riding on governments equipping themselves to kill large numbers of human beings.

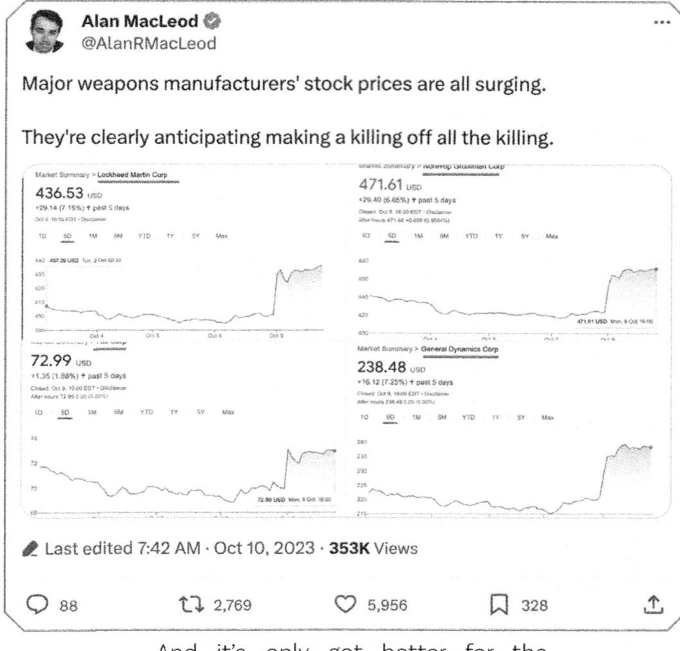

And it's only got better for the weapons industry since the writing of this article. Alan McLeod noted that the day the conflict in Israel kicked off sent military contractor's stock prices skyrocketing.

There's a popular quote, "It is no measure of health to be well-adjusted to a profoundly sick society," commonly attributed to Jiddu Krishnamurti but most likely coined by Kurt Vonnegut's son Mark. Whenever I read reports like this about corporations raking in billions from death, suffering, and extremely dangerous acts of brinkmanship between military powers, I always find that phrase "a profoundly sick society" rattling around in my head.

It's hard to imagine a society sicker than one in which corporations are not only allowed to profit from war and militarism, but to actually push for more of it using campaign donations, lobbying, and the funding of influential warmongering think tanks. It's no less evil than if corporations were allowed to slaughter foreigners like livestock and sell their body parts for profit at industrial scale; the only thing that's different is the payment plan. And yet the people who do this are celebrated as respected job creators instead of thrown into cages like the monsters they are.

This is not the sort of civilization we should strive to be well-adjusted to. It is no sign of health to be well-adjusted to a society in which someone can become a billionaire selling weapons of mass murder after lobbying the government to perpetrate those murders. It is no sign of health to be well-adjusted to a society in which the military industrial complex launders information through the media to promote its deadly products and agendas. It is no sign of health to be well-adjusted to a society in which war profiteering corporations can reap massive quarterly profits in a proxy war that was provoked by the west while pouring fortunes into think tanks which helped manufacture consent for those provocations and which spin the west's actions in a positive light for the media.

If this society could give rise to something so depraved as the military industrial complex, then it is not the sort of society we should seek to blend in with. This is the sort of society we should want to stick out like a sore thumb in. The sort of society in which we should be swimming against the current when everyone else is swimming with it. The sort of society in which we say a resounding NO to things that everyone else is saying yes to.

This society has failed as spectacularly as anything can possibly fail. We live in a mind-controlled dystopia where war profiteers get to steer public policy, where the entire biosphere is being fed into the wood chipper of global capitalism while we rapidly accelerate toward nuclear armageddon. This is the most insane civilization anyone could possibly design. We should seek dissent and divergence from it to the fullest extent possible.

•

On The Idiotic Notion That It's Brave To Support Nuclear Brinkmanship In Ukraine

During a Sunday appearance on Face the Nation to plug his new Zelensky movie, actor Sean Penn decried the "cowardice" of the US government in its caution around provoking a nuclear exchange with its proxy warfare in Ukraine.

"It is my absolute feeling that the caution with which the United States has pledged support, which seemed, in my reading of February 2022 was a, like a lean on in the fear of nuclear conflict, something I think all of us should look very carefully at and understand that, of course, is possible," Penn said. "And that's to be concerning. The likelihood is extremely low. And as one of our witnesses in the film says, you know, are we going to let a gangster with nuclear weapons dictate the way we live?"

Penn emotionally lamented the fact that the Biden administration did not pour F-16 warplanes into Ukraine from the very beginning of the conflict, initially fearing the move to be too escalatory. Describing this hesitation, Penn said that "at some point, caution becomes cowardice."

As you might expect, the interviewer refrained from challenging Penn on his claim that the likelihood of nuclear war is "extremely low" in spite of his acknowledgement that it's a real possibility, or on his claim that resisting increasing the likelihood of nuclear war is an act of cowardice.

Sean Penn has been one of Hollywood's most egregious empire apologists for some time now (in 2020 he told CNN that "there is no greater humanitarian force on the planet than the United States military"), but even by his standards these comments about nuclear brinkmanship are remarkably odious.

There's this obnoxious idea that comes up in mainstream political discourse about Ukraine that an aversion to nuclear brinkmanship is somehow cowardly, and that being willing to risk the life of every terrestrial organism advancing US strategic objectives is somehow an act of courage.

We saw this back in July from Paul Massaro, an advisor to the US government's Helsinki Commission and a minor celebrity in online Zelenskyite circles. During this year's "Captive Nations Summit" with the Victims of Communism Memorial Foundation, Massaro mocked westerners for being "fearful" of proxy warfare in Ukraine leading to nuclear warfare.

"I think the biggest thing is fear, I think we're fearful," Massaro said. "It's very funny to me, because you meet Ukrainians, not a single Ukrainian is fearful. You talk to Ukrainians it's like 'What if the Russians use nuclear weapons?', they're like 'We'll keep fighting, we'll win.' You know it's only the westerners that are like 'Oh my god, I'm over here in California and what if the Russians use nuclear weapons?' You know, it's almost pathetic."

It's a common theme. Any time you talk publicly about the risk of the continually escalating war in Ukraine leading to nuclear catastrophe you'll get empire apologists calling you a coward and saying we all need to be brave and stand up to the big bully Putin. And it's just such a disgusting perversion of what courage actually is and what it looks like.

Empire loyalists often talk about nuclear brinkmanship like it's something courageous that they personally are doing, as though gambling every terrestrial life on strategic grand chessboard maneuverings is a brave risk that could only hurt them. If you think you are brave for risking the life of everyone on earth to advance your personal geopolitical agendas, you might be a malignant narcissist, because you think the world revolves around you, and other lives exist only as props to support your main character adventures.

Hardly any human on this planet gives a shit who governs Crimea or the Donbass—and exactly zero of the plants and animals do—but people like Sean Penn and Paul Massaro think they have every right to not only gamble all their lives on a bid to control that outcome, but to call themselves courageous for doing so. Imagine being so self-absorbed you think you're a brave hero for putting the lives of Africans, Asians, and South Americans on the betting table who've never even heard of Donetsk or Luhansk and don't care who governs them, as well as every non-human life on earth.

I mean, the absolute arrogance. The fucking gall. It's as emotionally stunted and infantile a perspective as you could possibly come up with, but these are the people whose worldview is shaping outcomes on this planet. These are the sort of people who are setting the trajectory of our species as a collective.

The mainstream western political consensus is a sickness of the mind. Its existence should make us all want to fall to our knees and beg the forgiveness of every life on this earth that it imperils.

•

Barack Obama Belongs In A Fucking Cell

The Twitter account of America's 44th president just casually shared some links to organizations providing relief to the victims of the terrible flooding in Libya, which as of this writing has already killed thousands of people.

And that would of course be a fine and normal thing for America's 44th president to do—had America's 44th president not personally played a massive role in paving the way to the devastation we're seeing in Libya today.

"If you're looking to help people impacted by the floods in Libya, check out these organizations providing relief," Obama tweeted.

Uhh, excuse me? Sir? You know you're literally Barack Obama, right?

In 2010 the oil-rich Libya ranked higher on the UN Human Development Index than any other nation in Africa, with much better national infrastructure to protect itself from floods and other natural disasters. Today Libya is a chaotic humanitarian disaster where UN-backed investigators now say literal crimes against humanity have been taking place, including women being forced into sexual slavery.

What changed? If you're reading this, you probably already know what changed.

In 2011, US, French and British forces helped rebels with extensive links to Al Qaeda kill Libya's longtime leader Muammar Gaddafi, which immediately plunged the nation into violence, chaos, extremism and instability which persists to this day. It was later revealed that NATO powers knew they were backing murderous Al Qaeda-linked jihadists at the time.

Falsely branded a "humanitarian intervention" designed to prevent alleged plans for genocide and Viagra-fueled mass rapes against peaceful protesters by Gaddafi's troops, the NATO attack on Libya quickly morphed into a regime change operation which saw Gaddafi brutally lynched in the streets and dying after being stabbed in the anus with a bayonet. Years later in 2016 a UK House of Commons Foreign Affairs Committee found that the narratives used to justify the intervention in Libya were "not supported by the available evidence."

"We have seen no evidence that the UK Government carried out a proper analysis of the nature of the rebellion in Libya," the report reads. "UK strategy was founded on erroneous assumptions and an incomplete understanding of the evidence."

This confirmed concerns voiced by Amnesty International and a UN human rights investigator months before Gaddafi's death that the evidence for the alleged atrocities the intervention was meant to prevent simply wasn't there to be found. Because no policy changes were made after the Iraq invasion and nobody was ever punished for inflicting that horror upon our world, no lessons were learned, and it happened again. The west was deceived into yet another disastrous military intervention, which continues to have severe consequences for people in the region to this day.

In an article published earlier this month in Responsible Statecraft about the crisis in Niger, Branko Marcetic made the interesting observation that the Nigerien junta which ousted the previous government

has explicitly stated that the coup was necessary because of the "continuous deterioration of the security situation" which Niger and other countries in the Sahel have been suffering from for over a decade due to "the negative socioeconomic, security, political and humanitarian consequences of NATO's hazardous adventure in Libya."

Marcetic also notes that the regime change intervention in Libya was meant to segue into a regime change intervention in Syria by the same means:

"Sens. John McCain (R-Ariz.), Joe Lieberman (I-Conn.), and John Kerry (D-Mass.) all called for a no-fly zone. 'I love the military … but they always seem to find reasons why you can't do something rather than why you can,' complained McCain. The American Enterprise Institute's Danielle Pletka said it would be 'an important humanitarian step.' The now-defunct Foreign Policy Initiative (FPI) think tank gathered a who's who of neoconservatives to repeatedly urge the same. In a letter to then-President Barack Obama, they quoted back Obama's Nobel Peace Prize speech in which he argued that 'inaction tears at our conscience and can lead to more costly intervention later.'

"Then-Secretary of State Hillary Clinton, reportedly instrumental in persuading Obama to act, was herself swayed by similar arguments. Friend and unofficial adviser Sidney Blumenthal assured her that, once

Gaddafi fell, 'limited but targeted military support from the West combined with an identifiable rebellion' could become a new model for toppling Middle Eastern dictators. Pointing to the similar, deteriorating situation in Syria, Blumenthal claimed that 'the most important event that could alter the Syrian equation would be the fall of Gaddafi, providing an example of a successful rebellion.'"

And that's exactly what the Obama administration set out to do: pouring weapons into Syria with the goal of effecting regime change, once again on the side of Al Qaeda-linked fighters. Had Russia not intervened in 2015 to prevent Damascus from being toppled, Syria would likely have suffered the same fate as Libya.

So that's two countries Obama and his cohorts tossed in the incinerator back-to-back, in much the same way the previous administration torched Afghanistan and Iraq. It was done a bit more slyly and subtly than the overt Hulk Smash ground invasions of the Bush era, but the death, suffering and destabilization caused by Obama's depravity have been just as real.

This is as clear as day, and yet we still get imperial propaganda outlets like The Washington Post telling us that "everyone" is to blame for Libya's current troubles. WaPo has a new article out titled "Libya's catastrophe is everyone's fault," which is a bit like Charles Manson saying the Manson Family killings were everyone's fault.

The article's author Ishaan Tharoor lays the blame for Libya's inability to adequately protect its people from the flood on "Libya's feuding factions and fractured polity" as well as other nations in the region before conceding that NATO's toppling of Gaddafi would have also played some role.

Another Washington Post article titled "How a decade of conflict and division put Libya in peril of disaster" lays zero blame at all on Obama and NATO powers for the nation's suffering, saying only that Gaddafi was a brutal dictator who "was killed by rebel forces during a NATO-backed Arab Spring uprising." But it does acknowledge that Libyans are now dying because the nation's infrastructure has been in a state of decay since 2011:

"The country, with terrain ranging across desert and coastal communities, is highly vulnerable to human-induced climate change. But improvements to and maintenance of basic services and infrastructure, such as the country's networks of dams, has been deprioritized, said Mary Fitzgerald, a Libya expert at the Middle East Institute, a Washington think tank.

"'Between 2011 and 2014, there were already concerns about the state of Libyan infrastructure,' Fitzgerald said. 'And then Libya went through a six-year civil conflict from 2014 to 2020 and a lot of infrastructure was damaged during that conflict. In the three years since, you have a situation of rival government, which has yet again complicated political dynamics.'"

This nation has been in a continuous state of strife, violence and suffering since the United States spearheaded a NATO campaign to smash it to pieces. And yet you'll still get empire simps telling you that NATO is a "defensive alliance", and you'll still get liberals saying that Obama's worst scandal was wearing a tan suit one time.

Barack Obama belongs in a fucking cage. His crimes are utterly unforgivable, and if the law existed to punish the world's worst criminals instead of to protect them he would be rotting in a maximum security prison cell.

It's all well and good that people are sending Libya aid and that the call to do so is being amplified by influential voices. But the fact that the 44th president of the United States can just come out and pretend to support a nation he personally helped destroy without being called out and excoriated by the mass media shows that we live in a world which is dominated by lies and propaganda.

Featured image via NASA HQ PHOTO (CC BY-NC-ND 2.0)

If Everyone Understood That The US Deliberately Provoked The Ukraine War

War is the single worst thing humans do. The most insane. The most cruel. The most destructive. The most traumatic. The least sustainable. Those who knowingly choose to steer humanity into more war when it could be avoided are the worst people in the world, without exception.

And there are mountains of extensively documented evidence that that's exactly what the drivers of the US-centralized empire did in Ukraine. That's why so many western analysts and experts spent years warning that the actions of western powers were going to lead Ukraine into disaster, and it's why US empire managers keep openly boasting about how much their proxy warfare in Ukraine advances US interests. They knowingly steered Ukraine into war to advance their own geostrategic interests while being fully aware that no powerful nation would ever permit the kinds of foreign threats the west was amassing on its borders, and then they intervened in the early days of the war to prevent the outbreak of peace.

If there was widespread awareness of these facts, the US war machine would lose support around the world—not just for its actions in this one war, but for all future wars as well. Which is why so much energy goes into making sure this does not become a widespread understanding.

The official mainstream narrative throughout the western world is that Putin invaded Ukraine solely because he is evil and hates freedom. That's the actual, literal belief about this war that the western political/media class works to instill in the western public. Anyone who counters this self-evidently ridiculous assessment with facts and evidence gets branded a Russian agent and swarmed with pro-US trolls on social media, and loses all hope of securing a major platform in any mass media.

And it's important to notice that shutting down all mature adult analysis of the events which led to the war in this way does not actually save a single Ukrainian life. It doesn't make Russia any more likely to stop fighting and withdraw its troops. All it does is prevent people from seeing the US empire for what it really is. It isn't being done to protect Ukrainians, it's done to protect the empire.

The worst thing that could possibly happen to the information interests of the US empire would be for a critical mass of people to become aware that all this death and destruction in Ukraine could have been avoided by the US-centralized empire behaving less aggressively on Russia's doorstep, and that those aggressions were instead increased with the goal of advancing US strategic interests on the world stage. If everyone really, deeply understood that all this suffering, all these mountains of human corpses could simply not have happened if the US hadn't been feverishly focused on securing planetary domination at all cost, the US would no longer be able to manufacture consent for its agendas. It would no longer be able to whip up international support for its actions against its enemies. It would no longer be able to persuade the world to help prop up the hegemony of the dollar.

But because the US empire has the most advanced soft power apparatus that has ever existed, hardly anyone understands this. Not even the people who understand that the west provoked this war have deeply grappled with exactly what that means on a visceral emotional level, for the most part. It's more of a superficial intellectual understanding for most, without really grokking into the horror of it all, really letting the enraging nature of what the US empire did wash over them.

The west was deceived into supporting yet another evil American war, this time with the added dimension of nuclear brinkmanship threatening the life of every terrestrial organism. All to suck Moscow into another draining military quagmire so war plans can be safely drawn up against China while advancing US energy interests in Europe and building support for US military alliances. It's almost too evil to take in. There aren't really words for it.

And that's one of the reasons it's hard to get people to take in exactly what happened with Ukraine: people have a hard time wrapping their minds around the idea that **anyone** could be that evil, much less the government we've been trained by Hollywood to think of as sane and humanitarian.

It's about as monstrous a thing as you could possibly come up with. Yet here it is, still unfolding in all its blood-spattered glory.

Our task then is to help people see this and understand it, not just intellectually but emotionally. Help people really grasp deep down the horrors the US empire unleashed upon our world with the war in Ukraine; the suffering; the death; the existential danger. We can't fight the empire on our own, but we can each do what we can to help weaken the consent manufacturing machine it uses to rule and terrorize the world.

•

We Must Never Let Ourselves Become Desensitized To This

We must never let ourselves become desensitized to this. To any part of this.

We must never cease appreciating the sun on our skin and the wind in our hair, and we must never cease being shocked by the fact that there are people whose entire job is to push for more war.

We must never lose our sense of wonder at the birds in the air, and we must never lose our sense of horror at the fact that there are people who profit from war and militarism and lobby for more of it at every opportunity.

We must strive never to walk through a forest or a field or a parking garage or a shopping mall without being floored by the beauty we find there, and we must strive never to look at warmongering, ecocide, oppression and injustice without trembling with rage.

We must never allow ourselves to become so jaded and calloused that the rustling of leaves or bird songs fail to delight us, or that reading about starvation sanctions targeting civilian populations fails to draw hot tears of compassion from our eyes.

We mustn't let ourselves take for granted this boundless ocean of astonishing miracles we find ourselves swimming in—not even for an instant—and we mustn't let ourselves grow accustomed to any part of this freakishly abusive dystopia we were birthed into.

There's this weird taboo against expressing shock at the horrors of the empire, at the abuses, at the lies. Doing so often draws out a haughty, leaned-back response of, "Ha! That surprises you? I grew accustomed to that long ago."

This impulse is born of cowardice. It's so much easier to be jaded than to let it all in. So much easier to lean back smugly knowing better than to let yourself be brought to your knees in heartbreak. So much safer to hide out in world-weary cynicism than to let this world affect you in all its terrible glory.

But we lose so much when we let that callus build up, because there's no way to take the awfulness for granted without also doing the same with the wondrousness and the beauty. It all comes in through the same aperture within our perception, so it's impossible to inoculate yourself against experiencing the nightmare without also inoculating yourself against experiencing the ecstacy.

We've got to be brave enough to feel—to take it all in, the good and the bad. This doesn't mean responding unconsciously and becoming a rage addict drifting blindly through life on autopilot on the current of one's emotions, it means meeting life where it is, exactly as it is, without manipulating our experience of it to numb ourselves and give ourselves a sense of control.

That's what authentic living is, in my view: meeting life just as it is, without egocentric filters, distortions or manipulations, come what may. This is the only way to really live our time on this earth, to really experience each moment instead of missing it. It's also the only way for ordinary people to respond to tyranny and abuse with the emotional energy it requires.

Life-sized life. Beauty-flavored beauty. Carnage-colored carnage. It's all here, inviting us in to meet it on its terms, whenever we're ready.

Image via Adobe Stock

On Escalation, De-Escalation, And "Deterrence"

A very confused and distressed young man wandered into our home on Sunday and began acting erratically. He was clearly suffering from a severe mental illness, probably schizophrenia, and from his nice clothes yet disheveled appearance I'm guessing he had a home somewhere but had been on the street for a few days.

My husband Tim began talking to him and trying to figure out how to help him, but when Tim tried walking with him outside the man slammed the door on him and started raving about "recruiters" and saying Tim was a pedophile.

The man was too confused to figure out how to lock the door, so he was just leaning against it to keep Tim out. Tim's a big guy and a trained martial artist and could have forced his way back in and overpowered the man, but he also worked at a psychiatric facility for years and understood that this would needlessly escalate a situation that could probably be peacefully de-escalated.

Tim went around the back where I had just encountered the man and explained the situation to me in a calm and friendly way that would be sure not to agitate our unexpected houseguest. My family talked to him for a minute and he relaxed a bit, and then he left without a fuss.

Dave DeCamp ✔
@DecampDave

Deterrence in action

Antiwar.com ✔ @Antiwarcom · Sep 19
Taiwan Detects Record Number of Chinese Warplanes
China has significantly stepped up its military activity around Taiwan in response to growing US–Taiwan ties
by Dave DeCamp
@DecampDave #Taiwan #China ...
Show more

4:50 AM · Sep 19, 2023 · **2,606** Views

It was an interesting insight into this dynamic of escalation and de-escalation we see play out all around the world in various ways, from individual police interactions with the public to large-scale conflicts between world powers. A cop uses force on someone in the name of neutralizing a threat, the person becomes agitated by this escalation, starts fighting back, and gets killed by the cop. A superpower begins amassing war machinery near the border of its geopolitical rival in the name of deterring that rival from behaving aggressively, and the rival responds aggressively to that threat.

Anyone, regardless of their level of mental health, is going to feel threatened when weapons are pointed at them or violence is directed at them. The person pointing the weapons or directing the violence may sincerely feel that they are only defending themselves, but the other party will feel the same way, and may react with aggression to this escalation because they feel they've been put in a fight-or-die situation.

We know that's what happened with Ukraine. We know that's what's happening again with Taiwan, as we receive news of China ramping up its air force presence around the island in response to Taipei's increasing military intimacy with the United States. It's no longer seriously debatable that the strategy of surrounding a powerful nation with war machinery in the name of "deterrence" is actually extremely escalatory and leads to war.

The facts are in and the case is closed: amassing threats near the borders of powerful nations has an escalatory rather than de-escalatory effect. This is true of Russia and China, and history has shown us that it's true of the United States as well; the last time a credible military threat was placed near the US border, the US responded so aggressively that the world almost ended. If you still support this false "deterrence" strategy at this point after all the evidence is in, you're just a warmonger who wants a war.

There is a time and a place for violence, but that line is very, very far back from where most people tend to draw it. Violence and the threat thereof should always be a last resort, used only in self-defense, but we see police shooting people who move a little funny and the most powerful empire ever to exist waging constant wars of aggression and amassing more and more war machinery on the borders of its top two geopolitical opponents.

This isn't what should be happening. What should be happening is diplomacy, de-escalation and detente, with the ultimate goal being a world where governments work together for the good of everyone. There's no valid reason that can't happen.

It's usually possible to de-escalate tense situations just by talking it through. It can happen between global powers, it can happen in police interactions, and it can happen if a mentally ill person accidentally wanders into your home.

Image via Adobe Stock

The US Air Force Is Clearing Out Jungles In The Pacific To Prepare For War With China

The US Air Force is clearing out jungles in the Pacific and replacing them with
airfields for its coming war with China,
because there exist people on this earth who look at a jungle and think, "This
should be replaced with an airfield to prepare for a war with China."

There are people on this earth who say, "You know the world would be a much
better place if all these trees and exotic insects and birds were replaced with
long stretches of concrete lined with nuclear bombers on high alert."

There are people on this earth who see bulldozing rainforests to make way for
war planes as much simpler and easier than just making peace.

There are people on this earth who would spend their entire lives making
up new excuses to fight new enemies, and then tear up every inch of the
biosphere looking for ways to defeat those enemies.

There are people on this earth who would rather wipe out all biodiversity than
allow for any diversity in world leadership.

There are people on this earth who would rather rule supreme over a
wasteland of irradiated dust and ashes than see the rise of a multipolar
world.

There are people on this earth who would rather annihilate everything than
take a brief moment to pause and look inward.

There are people on this earth who would rather stare down the barrel of
nuclear armageddon than turn and stare at themselves.

There are people on this earth who would light the skies on fire before they'd
take even a minute to just be here now.

There are people on this earth who would rather destroy everything than make
peace with anything.

There are people on this earth who look at the staggering beauty of the
natural world and think how wonderful it would be if they could tear it all down
and funnel it into a factory to make Tomahawk missiles.

The biosphere is dying,
and we are hurtling toward nuclear war,
and it is so very, very heartbreaking,
and yet even in the midst of that heartbreak
nature shines as majestically as ever,
and some moments all you can do is take in the beauty
and take it as your solemn, sacred duty to appreciate it while it lasts,
and look at the trees and the bugs and the birds and the critters
who never had anything to do with this madness,
and bow as deeply as your body can bow,
and say I'm sorry.
I'm so sorry.

We're Being Prepared For The Ukraine War To Last Into The 2030s

Western officials and media pundits are now directly acknowledging that Ukraine's much-touted "spring counteroffensive" has been a catastrophic failure, but rather than seeing this as a reason to reconsider the mainstream political consensus on this war, they are instead telling everyone that the counteroffensive's failure means we must commit to the status quo of bloodshed and nuclear brinkmanship for years to come.

In a recent article titled "US and G-7 Allies Expect War in Ukraine to Drag On for Years," Bloomberg reports that the US-centralized power structure expects to be backing its proxy conflict against Russia for a very long time, potentially into the 2030s.

Bloomberg reports:

"The US and its allies in the Group of Seven now expect the war in Ukraine may drag on for years to come and are building that possibility into their military and financial planning.

"A senior official from one European G-7 country said the war may last as much as six or seven more years and that allies need to plan financially to continue support for Kyiv for such a long conflict.

"That's much longer than many officials had expected earlier this year, but slow progress in Ukraine's counteroffensive in recent months has tempered expectations."

In a recent interview with CNN, outgoing Joint Chiefs chair Mark Milley said that achieving Kyiv's official goal of fully recapturing all Ukrainian territory is going to require "very significant effort over a considerable amount of time."

"I can tell you that it'll take a considerable length of time to militarily eject all 200,000 or plus Russian troops out of Russian-occupied Ukraine," Milley added. "That's a very high bar. It's going to take a long time to do it."

In a recent interview with German newspaper Berliner Morgenpost, NATO Secretary General Jens Stoltenberg also pounded home the point that this war will drag on for a very long time.

"Most wars last longer than is expected when they first start. Therefore, we must prepare ourselves for a long war in Ukraine," Stoltenberg said.

"We are all wishing for a quick peace," Stoltenberg added. "But at the same time, we must recognize: If President Zelensky and the Ukrainians give up the fight, their country would not exist anymore. If President Putin and Russia laid down their weapons, we would have peace. The easiest way to end this war would be if Putin withdrew his troops."

You see this claim from empire managers and their apologists all the time: that the only obstacle to peace in Ukraine is Russia refusing to leave. This of course ignores the many extensively-documented western aggressions which are known to have provoked Russia's invasion, a fact that Stoltenberg himself admitted to earlier this month.

Demanding that Russia end its aggressions without the west agreeing to end its own aggressions which led to this conflict is just demanding that Russia lie down and submit to being ruled and dominated by the western empire. It's not a call for peace, it's a call for the total victory of Washington and its cohorts.

Stoltenberg reinforced his point that this war will drag on for years by affirming that Ukraine will gain NATO membership when this war is over, which is effectively a message to Moscow that if it still finds NATO membership for Ukraine unacceptable it must either annex Ukraine into the Russian Federation entirely or keep this war going on forever.

"Ukraine will become a member of NATO—all allies have made that clear," Stoltenberg said, adding that Ukraine will need NATO protection when the war ends, otherwise "history could repeat itself."

The western media are conveying the same message. Notorious empire propaganda rag The Economist has a new article out titled "Ukraine faces a long war. A change of course is needed," featuring a Ukrainian flag with the words "TIME FOR A RETHINK" scrawled across it. If you didn't know anything about The Economist you might assume at first glance that this was an article about rethinking the approach of backing an endless proxy conflict—especially after its opening paragraphs acknowledge that "The plan is not working" and "Ukraine has liberated less than 0.25% of the territory that Russia occupied in June."

You would be wrong though. What The Economist means is that we should switch from thinking of this as a war that can be won in a timely fashion to one which will continue for the foreseeable future:

"Both Ukraine and its Western supporters are coming to realise that this will be a grinding war of attrition. President Volodymyr Zelensky visited Washington this week for talks. 'I have to be ready for the long war,' he told The Economist. But unfortunately, Ukraine is not yet ready; nor are its Western partners. Both are still fixated on the counter-offensive. They need to rethink Ukraine's military strategy and how its economy is run. Instead of aiming to "win" and then rebuild, the goal should be to ensure that Ukraine has the staying power to wage a long war—and can thrive despite it."

So western empire managers and their agenda-setters in the mass media are making it as clear as could be that the US-centralized empire has found itself in yet another endless war, another "grinding war of attrition" featuring unfathomable destruction and suffering with no exit strategy, which once again pours vast fortunes into the coffers of the military industrial complex. The only difference is that this time it comes with the added bonus of the threat of nuclear annihilation.

All for what? To advance the US empire's goal of total planetary domination, a status quo that it can only maintain by brandishing armageddon weapons at its enemies with increasing hostility year after year.

When it comes to the war in Ukraine it is definitely time for a rethink, but not by the same monsters who thought us into this horror in the first place.

Featured image via NATO (CC BY-NC-ND 2.0)

This War Wasn't Just Provoked — It Was Provoked Deliberately

In an interesting speech about the way US imperial aggression provokes violence around the world, antiwar commentator Scott Horton made reference to an April 2022 article from Yahoo News that had previously escaped my attention.

The article is titled "In closer ties to Ukraine, U.S. officials long saw promise and peril," and it features named and unnamed veterans of the US intelligence cartel saying that long before the February 2022 invasion they were fully aware that the US had "provoked" Russia in Ukraine and created a powderkeg situation that would likely lead to war.

"By last summer [meaning the summer of 2021], the baseline view of most U.S. intelligence community analysts was that Russia felt sufficiently provoked over Ukraine that some unknown trigger could set off an attack by Moscow," a former CIA official told Yahoo News' Zach Dorfman, who adds, "(The CIA and the Office of the Director of National Intelligence declined to comment.)"

Dorfman writes that initial support provided to Ukraine during the Obama administration had been "calibrated to avoid aggravating Moscow," but that "partially spurred by Congress, as well as the Trump administration, which was more willing to be aggressive on weapon transfers to Kyiv, overt U.S. military support for Ukraine grew over time—and with it the risk of a deadly Russian response, some CIA officials believed at the time."

Policymakers "would always say, 'If we do X thing, if we give the Ukrainians X system, how are the Russians going to react?' And our answer would always be, 'You can't look at any one thing in isolation,'" the unnamed former CIA official told Yahoo News. "And we might look and say, 'Well, it's just a few hundred MANPADs [man-portable air-defense systems] or a few hundred Humvees,' but it's missing the point that the Russians are taking all of this stuff in the aggregate, and they're drawing this picture of this ever-increasing relationship between the U.S. and Ukraine."

"I understand the moral argument," says former CIA official Jeffrey Edmonds regarding the weapons transfers into Ukraine, "but I also understand the argument that, well, why would you want to give these things if it's just going to increase the chances that Russia does something?"

So while we members of the public were blindly speculating about whether or not Russia would attack Ukraine, the US intelligence cartel was fully aware that the US was taking actions ensuring that that would happen. That's the environment the US security state knew it was operating under when it continued to taunt the idea of adding Ukraine and Georgia to NATO right up until the final moments before the invasion.

This war wasn't just provoked, it was knowingly provoked. Off ramp after off ramp was sped past by the US war machine at a hundred miles an hour on its beeline toward a horrific proxy war, because empire managers had calculated that such a war would serve US interests. And now we routinely see US officials like Mitch McConnell openly saying that this war serves US interests.

They really couldn't be more obvious about it if they tried.

It's been funny to watch the response of empire apologists to NATO Secretary General Jens Stoltenberg's surprising refutation of a year and a half of empire propaganda by openly admitting that NATO expansion provoked the invasion of Ukraine and acknowledging that NATO powers rejected Moscow's proposed compromises which could have averted the war. Basically the only argument they now have after this admission is to say that Russia should not have viewed NATO expansion as an existential threat.

Their only remaining trick is to argue with reality; to basically say that yes it's reality that NATO expansion provoked this war because Moscow saw it as a threat, but reality shouldn't have been what reality was. They argue that Russia should have felt completely different feelings about a military threat on its border than nations like the United States would feel, since as we've discussed previously the last time there was a credible military threat near the US border the US responded so aggressively that the world almost ended.

That's really all they've got: "Yes it's true that all the people who've died and lost their homes in this war did so because we were amassing a hostile military alliance near Russia's border,

but in our defense the Russians should've thought different thoughts in their heads than the ones that we ourselves would think about a hostile military threat on our border."

If all westerners deeply understood all the suffering and danger that has been unleashed upon our world by this war, and deeply understood the fact that their own governments played a role in starting it, the political status quo of the western world would be impossible to maintain. Which is why such unprecedented levels of propaganda and internet censorship have gone into preventing westerners from coming to such an understanding.

Westerners were deceived into supporting yet another evil war, which once again is showing every sign of dragging on for the foreseeable future with no exit strategy in sight. The only difference between this war and all those other wars is that this one is laden with the risk of nuclear annihilation, a risk which the US empire has been treading less and less carefully around as the bloodshed continues.

The more you think about it, the more horrifying it gets.

These people are absolute monsters.

Featured image via Global Panorama (CC BY-SA 2.0)

American State Propaganda: A Thought Experiment

The New York Times has published another CIA press release disguised as news, this time aimed at whipping up paranoia toward anyone who criticizes the US proxy war in Ukraine.

The article is titled "Putin's Next Target: U.S. Support for Ukraine, Officials Say". Its author, Julian E Barnes, has written so many New York Times articles with headlines ending in the words "Officials Say" that we can safely assume the primary reason for his continued employment in that paper is because empire managers within the US government have designated him someone who can be trusted to print what they want printed. This designation would make him a reliable supplier of "scoops" (read: regurgitations of unevidenced government claims) for The New York Times.

"American officials said they are convinced that Mr. Putin intends to try to end U.S. and European support for Ukraine by using his spy agencies to push propaganda supporting pro-Russian political parties and by stoking conspiracy theories with new technologies," Barnes writes.

Of course the report never gets any more specific than that, and of course the "American officials" Barnes cites promote their unevidenced assertions under cover of complete anonymity.

"The American officials spoke on the condition their names not be reported so they could discuss sensitive intelligence," Barnes writes.

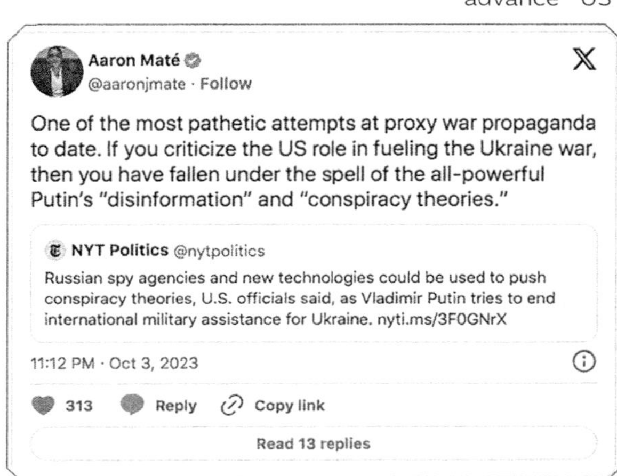

The only named source cited in the article is a CIA veteran named Beth Sanner, who says that "Russia will not give up on disinformation campaigns," but adds that "we don't know what it is going to look like."

And that's really the whole article right there. Putin is going to be using his spy agencies to promote political parties and messages which support ending the practice of pouring billions of dollars of weapons into Ukraine, but nobody knows what that will look like exactly, so we all have to just be sort of generally distrustful toward anyone who doesn't think it's a swell idea to perpetuate a horrific war with potentially world-ending consequences, because they might be part of an unspecified Russian influence operation.

We saw a similar report from CNN a few weeks ago, in which the public was warned that Russia's FSB is working to convert westerners into mouthpieces for Russian propaganda using methods so sneaky and subtle that those westerners wouldn't even know it's happening. Again, details were extremely vague and the only obvious response to the information provided is for everyone to just get really paranoid toward anyone saying anything that doesn't support current US foreign policy toward Russia.

As a thought experiment, imagine what it would look like if the CIA or some other agency wanted to advance US information interests by making the public distrustful of any people or information which go against US strategic objectives. Try to imagine some of the things they might say or do.

Do you imagine it would look much different than what we're seeing currently? Feeding trusted mainstream news reporters extremely vague stories about the Kremlin trying to deceive people into opposing the longstanding agendas of the US intelligence cartel, using online media and social subversion? Can you think of a more effective way to help shore up trust in your preferred narratives and sow distrust in narratives you do not prefer?

Here's another one: imagine a state media outlet for a tyrannical dictatorship. Think about how its news stories are made, how it would often take orders from the government on what to report and what not to report, and how all its printing or broadcasting would always align with the information interests of that government.

Now ask yourself: in what material way is that reporting different from these CIA press releases we're seeing from outlets like The New York Times and CNN? In both scenarios the government is feeding the media information it wants printed, and in both scenarios there will be consequences if the media don't obey. In our hypothetical dictatorship those consequences might be more severe, but in our real life scenario the consequences are no less real.

If Mr Barnes had refused to work on this story, he would have lost his "scoop" and it would have been given to someone else, perhaps at a competing outlet. If Barnes ceased uncritically reporting unevidenced assertions from anonymous government officials, his prominence in the mainstream media would quickly fizzle, and his career would dry up. If The New York Times ceased functioning as a reliable outlet for the credulous printing of unevidenced government claims, then the government agencies who've been elevating the paper to prominence with their artificial "scoops" can take those hot stories to another competing outlet and let them get the subscriptions and the glory.

In both scenarios, the government is able to get its propaganda messaging printed as hard news reporting. In one scenario the reporter reports what the government wants because they work for the government, in the other scenario the reporter reports what the government wants because that's the only way to have a career in media outlets that are owned and controlled by the plutocrats who benefit from the political status quo the government is premised upon. The only major difference is that in our hypothetical dictatorship, the public probably knows it's being fed propaganda, and is therefore more likely to take what they're being told with a grain of salt.

In a tyrannical dictatorship, the press is operated by employees of the government. In a Free Democracy™, the press is operated by employees of the oligarchs who operate the government. In both cases you're getting state propaganda, but in one of them the propaganda is disguised as objective news reporting.

Image via Adobe Stock

The Mad Propaganda Push To Normalize War Profiteering In Ukraine

There's been an astonishingly brazen propaganda push to normalize war profiteering in Ukraine as Kyiv coordinates with the arms industry and western governments to convert the war-ravaged nation into a major domestic weapons manufacturer, thereby turning Ukrainians into proxies of the military industrial complex as well as the Pentagon.

At an event in Kyiv which hosted 250 "defense" industry corporations from 30 different countries on Friday, President Zelensky gave a speech urging war profiteers to open factories in Ukraine to cut out the middleman of securing and delivering so many weapons from abroad. This is an investment that the arms industry would ostensibly have plenty of time to set up, given that western officials are now going out of their way to communicate to the public that this war will stretch on for many more years to come.

Zelensky's speech twice made use of the phrase "defense-industrial complex", and used the phrase "arsenal of the free world" no fewer than three times.

"Ukraine is developing a special economic regime for the defense-industrial complex," Zelensky said. "To give all the opportunities to realize their potential to every company that works for the sake of defense—in Ukraine and with Ukraine or that wants to come to Ukraine."

"Right now, the most powerful military-industrial complexes are being determined, as are their priorities and the global standard of defense. All of this is being determined in Ukraine," Zelensky tweeted with photos from the event.

This move has been accompanied in recent weeks by some of the most appalling mass media headlines that I've ever seen, all geared toward normalizing the military industrial complex in the eyes of the public.

In an amazingly awful Wall Street Journal op-ed titled titled "In Defense of the Defense Industry" and subtitled "Populists of the right and left attack U.S. companies that make weapons. Who do they think protects us?", Future of Capitalism's Ira Stoll argues that the military industrial complex is actually a wonderful thing we should all love and support.

"The weapons industry protects America and its allies, keeping us safe from ruthless enemies who would otherwise exterminate or enslave us," Stoll writes. "Raytheon helps make weapons systems that defend Israeli civilians against attacks from Iran-backed terrorist groups. These include the Iron Dome, David's Sling, SkyHunter interceptor systems and Tamir missiles. Raytheon also produces the Javelin antitank missile that Ukraine has used against Russian armor and the early-warning radars that would detect incoming missiles aimed at the U.S."

Stoll does not name the alternate universe he is describing in which the US military is used to keep Americans

safe rather than to advance imperial interests abroad.

Another recent Wall Street Journal article titled "The War in Ukraine Is Also a Giant Arms Fair" and subtitled "Arms makers are getting orders for weapons being put to the test on the battlefield" glorifies the way war machinery is being field tested on human bodies to the benefit of war profiteers.

"The Panzerhaubitze howitzer is part of an arsenal of weapons being put to the test in Ukraine in what has become the world's largest arms fair," writes WSJ's Alistair MacDonald. "Companies that make the weapons being used in Ukraine have won orders and resurrected production lines. The deployment of billions of dollars worth of equipment in a major land war has also given manufacturers and militaries a unique opportunity to analyze the battlefield performance of weapons, and learn how best to use them."

A Reuters article from two weeks ago titled "At London arms fair, global war fears are good for business" gushes over how much money is being raked in by arms manufacturers as a result of this war, with one unnamed arms industry executive telling Reuters, "War is good for business."

Just the other day CNN anchor Erin Burnett followed up some clips of "far right lawmakers" voicing their opposition to funding for the Ukraine proxy war by pausing to explain to her audience that this funding is actually good for Americans, because it goes straight into the US arms industry.

"It's worthwhile with all of this gaining some steam in public perception to be clear on some facts," Burnett said. "First and foremost, the vast majority of this money is going to American companies and jobs, right, because those are the people that

are making the Abrams tanks, the ammo and everything else. And you take Lockheed Martin, which makes the HIMARS, that have been core to Ukraine's counteroffensive, the company announced it's going to increase its workforce in Camden, Arkansas, by 20 percent, just because of this new demand."

"That money is going to America," Burnett added.

All this propaganda energy is going into normalizing the act of war profiteering because if you let the idea stand on its own, it would make people scream in horror. The fact that a deliberately-provoked war is being used as a giant field demo to show prospective buyers and investors how effective various weapons systems can be at ripping apart human bodies in order to profit from all this death and destruction is more nightmarish than anything any dystopian novelist has ever come up with.

Ukraine is a giant advertisement for weapons of mass slaughter, and the cost of that corporate ad is not money but human blood. If you look right at this thing it absolutely chills you to the bone. Which is why so much effort is being poured into making sure people don't look at it.

Image via Adobe Stock

Everyone Wants Change And Nobody Wants To Change

An unspoken premise of capitalism is that one day people will invent some technology which allows humanity to keep consuming at a frenetic pace and keep expanding the economy without destroying the biosphere we depend on for survival. That's the only way to make capitalism look like a sustainable model for our planet.

But that isn't going to happen. We're never going to consume our way out of the ecosystemic problems we consumed our way into. Technology has helped our species in many ways, and will continue to, but no amount of technological innovation is going to make it possible to continue infinite economic expansion on a finite planet with finite resources and an ability to absorb a finite amount of disruption.

Human behavior itself is what needs to change—and it needs to change drastically, and it needs to change soon. No amount of technological innovation will ever circumvent that urgent need. We're like a smack addict trying to figure out ways they can keep using at a high volume without compromising their relationships and employment. We're like a miserable narcissist believing he can become happy if everyone in his life changes to accommodate his inner demons and facilitate his happiness.

Everyone wants change and nobody wants to change. But that is what's being asked of us. In the age of Bernays capitalism shifted from a need-based economy to a desire-based economy which tugs at the strings of the ego to fuel an insatiable drive to consume and produce and reject contentment with the way things are, and we're going to have to uproot what those strings are attached to in order to survive. Believing human consciousness can remain chained to these frenetic egoic patterns which drive us to consume and hoard and flail around in a constant state of restlessness and discontentment without destroying the biosphere if we can only come up with the right clever new trick is just a form of spiritual bypassing to avoid doing the real work that needs to get done in ourselves.

Our species has come to its adaptation-or-extinction juncture in its development on this planet, and the adaptation that's being asked for is a drastic change in human consciousness. We're going to have to grow up and become a conscious species now. Daddy Technology isn't coming to our rescue. It's on us. It's time to wake up and free ourselves from the dream of egoic consciousness so we can begin collaborating with each other and with our ecosystem toward a healthy and harmonious world.

.

It's Hard To Find Fulfillment In A Civilization That Revolves Around Corporate Profits

It's so hard to live as an authentic human being in a civilization whose every molecule is wrapped around something as vapid and soulless as corporate profit.

It's what most of us pour most of our life force into. Most people work all day generating corporate profits to pay bills that go toward corporate profits and pay off loans from giant banks for their corporate profits or rent from real estate giants for their corporate profits. Then they come home, eat some products from giant megacorporations that they purchased at a supermarket chain, and unwind by watching entertainment created by corporations to draw as many eyeballs as possible or scrolling through social media platforms designed by corporations to be as addictive as possible. We do this while being surrounded all day by advertising designed to pull us into generating more corporate profits.

Corporate profits are our life. Corporate profits are our religion. Most of us pour more of our energy into generating corporate profits throughout our lives than the most pious monk pours into worshipping any deity. Not because we want to, but because we have to. We were born into this bizarre civilization where everything revolves around corporate profits instead of love, relationships, connection, thriving, purpose, or personal depth.

Is it any wonder then that so many of us are suffering from addictions and depression and anxiety? I mean, how could we not be? Take a normal healthy human animal and throw it into the mess of this dystopian corporate nightmare and tell me how it's meant to live a happy and satisfying life. It's like expecting dolphins and orcas to live happy and satisfying lives in concrete pools at theme parks, or factory farmed pigs living in cages barely bigger than their bodies. It's just not the kind of living we're built for.

The blink of an eye ago our ancestors were hunter-gatherers living off the land, spending most of their waking lives under the open sky. Now all of a sudden we're expected to sit eight hours a day in a cubicle staring at screens for no other reason than to help the corporation that employs us increase its profits, then commute home under a barrage of advertising in a vehicle made by a corporation using fuels extracted by a corporation, and spend all our free time feeding into the profits of other corporations. Everything in us is screaming that this is insane and unacceptable.

That's why some people try to spend time in nature; it's one of the few ways you can get your head above all the corporate bullshit for a bit and take a few desperate breaths of what it's like to be a normal human organism. "Nature" used to just be "the world"; there was no other, separate thing from nature that we spent all our time in, pouring all our life force into, dedicating all our thoughts and feelings to, from whence we could escape for a few hours on the weekend as a luxury. Now we live in civilization and sneak out every now and then into this other thing, nature, where screens aren't blaring at us and the trees don't speak the language of the babbling narratives in our heads—though, if we're honest with ourselves, our minds are still mostly preoccupied with the pushing and pulling demands that civilization makes of us the entire time.

The only way to live in this civilization without its madness warping you and twisting you in on yourself is to change your relationship with mental narrative to such an extent that you can recognize that civilization is nature—that the human animal and its products are not separate from anything else in this biosphere we arose from. With a fair amount of dedicated inner work one can come to recognize that this sea of language we exist in is just narrative that we don't need to invest any of our life force in believing, and that all the words and thoughts are just energy like all the rest of nature.

From that point of view, a busy office full of chattering humans is not experientially much different from a busy forest full of chattering birds and insects—it's just two different expressions of nature. An advertisement is not experientially much different from crashing waves—it's just the sights and sounds of nature taking different energetic shapes. If you're not imbuing any of the narratives inside or outside of your head with the power of belief, it's all just a beautiful expression of nature.

That's the only way to live as a happy and healthy human organism in this civilization, from my point of view. Everything else is just varying degrees of insanity. Adjusting from an unwholesome relationship with mental narrative to a wholesome one lets you live a happy and fulfilling life among the humans, who are actually a staggeringly beautiful and thrilling animal when you can see them with fresh eyes.

And, as an added benefit, changing your relationship with narrative will greatly aid you in seeing through the consent-manufacturing propaganda that's used by the powerful to keep the dysfunctionality of this civilization going. If enough people snap out of their unhealthy relationship with narrative, a healthy world will suddenly become possible.

Image by Adobe Stock

They're Repeating The Word 'Unprovoked' Again, This Time In Defense Of Israel

Illusory truth effect

文ₐ **12 languages** ⌄

Article Talk

Read Edit View history Tools ⌄

From Wikipedia, the free encyclopedia

⊕

The **illusory truth effect** (also known as the **illusion of truth effect**, **validity effect**, **truth effect**, or the **reiteration effect**) is the tendency to believe false information to be correct after repeated exposure.[1] This phenomenon was first identified in a 1977 study at Villanova University and Temple University.[2][3] When truth is assessed, people rely on whether the information is in line with their understanding or if it feels familiar. The first condition is logical, as people compare new information with what they already know to be true. Repetition makes statements easier to process relative to new, unrepeated statements, leading people to believe that the repeated conclusion is more truthful. The illusory truth effect has also been linked to hindsight bias, in which the recollection of confidence is skewed after the truth has been received.

We're seeing the western political/media class bleating the word "unprovoked" in unison again, this time in reference to the massive multi-pronged operation launched by Hamas against Israel on Saturday morning which reportedly killed hundreds of Israelis.

"The United States unequivocally condemns the **unprovoked** attacks by Hamas terrorists against Israeli civilians," reads a statement from the White House.

"The loss of life in Israel as a result of the violent, calculated and **unprovoked** attack by Hamas is heartbreaking," reads a statement by House Minority Leader Hakeem Jeffries.

"The **unprovoked** terror attack today and the murders of innocent Israeli citizens are a stark reminder of the brutality of Hamas and Iran-backed extremists," reads a statement by congressman and house speaker contender Jim Jordan.

"This ignominious, **unprovoked**, and barbaric attack on Israel must be met with world condemnation and unequivocal support for the Jewish state's right to self-defense," tweeted presidential candidate Robert F Kennedy Jr.

"This is an '**unprovoked** attack on civilians': Lt. Gen. Keith Kellogg," reads a recent Fox News report.

"**Unprovoked** aggression by Hamas terrorists," reads a tweet by former secretary of state Mike Pompeo.

"I forcefully condemn these cowardly, horrifying, **unprovoked** attacks on Israel by Hamas," tweeted congressman John Fetterman.

"These attacks by Hamas against Israel were heinous and **unprovoked**," tweeted Senator Mark Kelly.

"As a steadfast supporter and ally of Israel, I unequivocally condemn the **unprovoked** and unprecedented terrorist attack launched by Hamas and stand with the people of Israel as it rightly defends itself," tweeted congressman Richie Torres.

"The **unprovoked** attacks on Israel by Hamas through Gaza and via air and sea, are absolutely a terrorist attack," tweeted Democratic Party pundit Ed Krassenstein.

"I unequivocally condemn Hamas' horrific, **unprovoked** attacks and call on all parties to take steps to prevent civilian harm," tweeted congresswoman Sara Jacobs.

I could cite many, many more examples, but I think that's enough to make the point I'm trying to make. Isn't it strange seeing the same oddly specific word choice inserted over and over and over again about the same event in statements by politicians and pundits, regardless of their political affiliation? When you lay them all out together it starts to sound highly suspicious, like someone always referring to his car as "my car, which I did not steal," or always introducing his spouse as "my wife, whom I do not beat."

It's clear by now that whenever you see the word "unprovoked" being forcefully repeated in a uniform way across the entire political/media class, whatever they're talking about was definitely massively provoked.

We saw this exact same thing when Russia invaded Ukraine; from the very beginning western politics and media were saturated with the word "unprovoked", bashing the western public in the face with that message over and over and over again despite the obvious and undeniable fact that the war in Ukraine was most definitely provoked.

As Noam Chomsky quipped last year, "Of course, it was provoked. Otherwise, they wouldn't refer to it all the time as an unprovoked invasion."

And the same is of course true of the latest Hamas offensive. There are all kinds of arguments you could legitimately make about it, but one argument you definitely cannot defend is that it was unprovoked. As Palestinian-American writer and comedian Amer Zahr put it on Twitter, "75 years of ethnic cleansing. 15 years of blockade. Confiscation of Palestinian lands. Pogroms on Palestinian towns. Desecration of Palestinian sacred sites. Daily raids into Palestinian homes. Constant humiliation of a entire people. Nothing about today is 'unprovoked.'"

Calling Palestinian violence against Israel "unprovoked" is easily even more ridiculous than calling the Russian invasion unprovoked, because the abuses of Israeli apartheid are so well-known by the general public at this point. Multiple mainstream human rights organizations have accused Israel of administering an abusive apartheid regime which treats Palestinians as lesser people. Palestinians who live in the open-air prison known as Gaza are deliberately subjected to undrinkable water, food shortages, energy shortages and bombing campaigns. Those outside Gaza are subjected to racist, violent policing and land seizure and live under a different set of laws than Jewish Israelis. The entire people were forced out of their homes to make way for a new state for reasons that had nothing to do with them, and any attempt to resist this has seen them killed as "terrorists".

Of course the attack was provoked.

Isn't it odd that the western political/media class would begin uniformly asserting something so easily disprovable? So transparently false? Why would they keep choosing over and over and over again in each instance to make use of that specific word "unprovoked" in their condemnations of the attacks by Hamas?

The answer is that this choice is not so much something they are saying as something they are doing. They're not attempting to communicate with their audiences, they're attempting to circumvent the critical thinking of their audience and trick them into accepting a blatant falsehood as true.

Skillful manipulators make frequent use of a cognitive bias known as the illusory truth effect, a glitch in the way human minds tend to operate which makes it hard for us to differentiate between the experience of hearing a well-evidenced fact and the experience of hearing something that they've heard repeated multiple times. If you want the public to believe something false you won't be able to use facts and evidence to make your case to them, so what you can do is just repeat something over and over again until it starts sounding like the truth. Repeat the lie enough times and boom, you've perception-managed westerners into viewing the world from an understanding that Israel did nothing to provoke Palestinians into their actions.

After the news broke about the Hamas offensive I tweeted, "Here come days and days of western news media slyly reversing the aggressor-defender relationship and reporting as though the violence began with the Hamas offensive, spontaneously out of nowhere."

But even I wasn't expecting the perception management to be this brazen.

•

Crazy, Unrealistic People Vs Rational, Realistic People

Crazy, unrealistic people believe all our systems are rigged for the benefit of the rich and powerful.

Rational, realistic people believe all our systems happen to benefit the rich and powerful by pure coincidence.

Crazy, unrealistic people believe the mass media feed the public lies to manufacture consent for agendas which go against public interests.

Rational, realistic people believe the media are telling the truth, and the public just naturally enjoys supporting wars on the other side of the planet and domestic policies which make them poorer and sicker.

Crazy, unrealistic people believe drastic, revolutionary changes are needed to create a just society which works for everyone.

Rational, realistic people believe a just society that works for everyone can be achieved by participating in political parties that are explicitly set up to prevent a just society that works for everyone.

Crazy, unrealistic people believe drastic revolutionary changes are needed in our society to avoid an environmental collapse that is already well underway.

Rational, realistic people believe the environmental collapse that is already well underway can be avoided by making small, incremental changes over the next several centuries.

Crazy, unrealistic people believe the US empire has lied about its every war, and is also lying about the current one.

Rational, realistic people believe that while history has shown that the US lied about all those other wars, this time it's definitely telling the truth.

Crazy, unrealistic people believe the US empire amassing war machinery on the borders of its top two geopolitical rivals is an extremely provocative act of aggression designed to advance the empire's geostrategic objectives.

Rational, realistic people believe the US amassing war machinery on the borders of its top two geopolitical rivals is an innocent act of defense.

Crazy, unrealistic people believe government agencies are spying on us and working to censor the internet.

Rational, realistic people believe that too, but they think it's a good thing.

Crazy, unrealistic people believe a status quo of nonstop war, militarism, nuclear brinkmanship, ecocide, exploitation, oppression and authoritarianism is untenable, and must be dismantled by any means necessary.

Rational, realistic people believe we can just ignore those problems and think about more pleasant things.

Crazy, unrealistic people believe that the only way to achieve desperately needed change in a society whose systems are rigged for the powerful is to disregard those rigged systems and use the power of our numbers to force the end of the injustices we face and the creation of new systems.

Rational, realistic people believe we can get the changes we need if we just vote a little harder in the next election.

Crazy, unrealistic people believe the definition of insanity is continually doing the same thing over and over and expecting different results.

Rational, realistic people believe doing the same thing over and over and expecting different results just might work this time.

Featured image via B Rosen (CC BY-ND 2.0)

Bill Kristol's Refreshingly Honest Ukraine War Ad

The Bill Kristol-led group "Republicans for Ukraine" has released a TV ad to help drum up GOP support for Washington's proxy war against Russia, and it's surprisingly honest about what this war is really about: advancing US strategic interests using Ukrainians as sacrificial pawns.

Here's a transcript:

> "When America arms Ukraine, we get a lot for a little. Putin is an enemy of America. We've used 5% of our defense budget to arm Ukraine, and with it, they've destroyed 50% of Putin's Army. We've done all this by sending weapons from storage, not our troops. The more Ukraine weakens Russia, the more it also weakens Russia's closest ally, China. America needs to stand strong against our enemies, that's why Republicans in Congress must continue to support Ukraine."

"Republicans for Ukraine" was launched last month by "Defending Democracy Together", another Kristol-led narrative management operation which is funded by oligarchs like Pierre Omidyar. Kristol, who as a neoconservative thought leader played a pivotal role in pushing for the 2003 invasion of Iraq, tweeted on Saturday that the ad "will air on the Sunday shows tomorrow in DC."

One of the dumbest things the empire asks us to believe is that this war simultaneously (A) was completely unprovoked and (B) just coincidentally happens to massively advance the strategic interests of the government accused of provoking it. From the moment Russia invaded Ukraine in February 2022 westerners were aggressively hammered over and over and over again by the mass media with the uniform propaganda message that this was an "unprovoked invasion", but ever since then we've also been receiving these peculiar messages from US empire managers and spinmeisters that this war is helping the United States crush its geopolitical enemies and advance its interests abroad.

This bizarre two-step occurs because the US-centralized empire needs to convey two self-evidently contradictory messages to the public at all times:

1. that the US is an innocent little flower who just wants to help its good friends the Ukrainians protect their democracy from the murderous Russians who invaded solely because they are evil and hate freedom, and

2. that it's in the interest of Americans to continue this war.

The second point is required because the message that the US is merely an innocent passive witness to the violence in Ukraine necessarily causes certain political factions to ask, "Okay, so what are we doing there then? Why are we pouring all this money into something that has nothing to do with us?" So another narrative is required to explain that backing this proxy war also just so happens to be a massive boon to US strategic interests abroad while creating American jobs manufacturing weapons at home.

And of course this war advances US strategic interests. Of course it does. Only an idiot would believe the US is pouring weapons into another country because it loves the people who live there and wants them to be free, and that it is only by pure coincidence that this happens to kill a lot of Russians, bolster NATO, and advance US energy interests in Europe. It doesn't benefit normal Americans at home, but it absolutely does serve the interests of the globe-spanning empire that's centralized around Washington. That's why the empire deliberately provoked it.

Empire managers were openly discussing the ways a war in Ukraine would directly benefit the US empire long before the invasion. In 2019 a Pentagon-funded Rand Corporation paper titled "Extending Russia—Competing from Advantageous Ground" detailed how the empire can use proxy warfare, economic warfare and other Cold War tactics to push its longtime geopolitical foe to the brink without costing American lives or sparking a nuclear conflict. The US Army-commissioned paper mentioned Ukraine hundreds of times, and explicitly discussed how a war there could be used to promote sanctions against Moscow and attack Russia's energy interests in Europe.

In December of 2021 John Deni of NATO propaganda firm The Atlantic Council authored a piece for The Wall Street Journal titled "The Strategic Case for Risking War in Ukraine," subtitled "An invasion would be a diplomatic, economic and military mistake for Putin. Let him make it if he must." Deni argued that "there are good strategic reasons for the West to stake out a hard-line approach" against Moscow and refuse to negotiate or back down over Ukraine, because if doing so provokes Russia to invade it would "forge an even stronger anti-Russian consensus across Europe," "result in another round of more debilitating economic sanctions that would further weaken Russia's economy," and "sap the strength and morale of Russia's military while undercutting Mr. Putin's domestic popularity and reducing

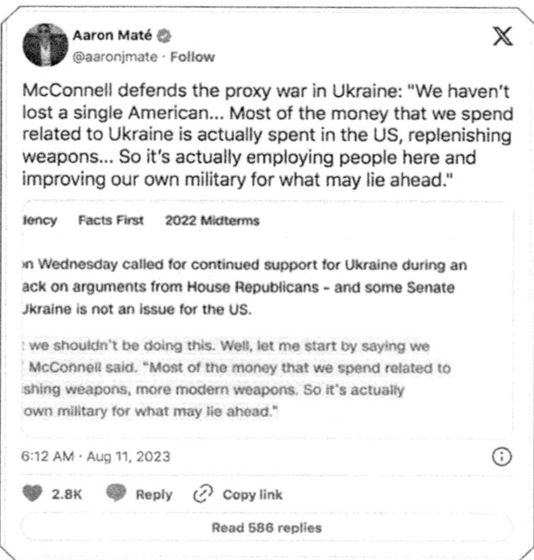

Russia's soft power globally."

The minds on the inside of the empire were talking about how this war would benefit the US before the invasion, and they've been talking about how much it benefits the US ever since. As the Washington Post's David Ignatius put it this past July: "these 18 months of war have been a strategic windfall, at relatively low cost (other than for the Ukrainians). The West's most reckless antagonist has been rocked. NATO has grown much stronger with the additions of Sweden and Finland. Germany has weaned itself from dependence on Russian energy and, in many ways, rediscovered its sense of values. NATO squabbles make headlines, but overall, this has been a triumphal summer for the alliance."

The managers of the empire are getting everything they want out of this war. In public they rend their garments and cry crocodile tears and call it a terrible criminal atrocity, but every now and then they look at the camera and flash it a quick Fleabag-style grin.

They knew exactly what they were doing when they provoked this war, and they know exactly what they're doing by keeping it going.

And they're loving every minute of it.

Image using Adobe Stock

Relish The Gaps

"I'm sorry… do you need your nurse?" I said, reluctantly giving her my hand to hold.

Her bones felt frail. I wasn't there to see her. I didn't know this woman.

"Everyone lets life pass them by," she said urgently, ignoring my obvious discomfort. "They're always focused on attaining and accomplishing, meeting their goals, winning people's approval. Then before they know it they're sitting in a place like this, wondering where it all went."

"I'll tell you where it all went," she continued, cutting me off before I could reply. "It zipped right past them while their minds were wrapped up in the next thing. The next event. The next goal. The next accomplishment. Then it's all over, and all they've got is a handful of memories of those few things they were focused on, with all the gaps gone unnoticed and unappreciated."

"The gaps?" I said.

"Yes the gaps child, the gaps in between! In between all those moments they spent their lives looking forward to. That's where all the life is!"

She smiled and gave my hand a little pat before relaxing back into her chair. Her exertion had taken it out of her.

"Or almost all of it, anyways. All those moments where you're sitting, walking, working, talking, seeing, hearing, feeling, smelling. Everyone lets them pass them by while they're focused on other things. They don't relish them. They don't enjoy them as they come. It's disrespectful, really."

"Disrespectful?"

"Yes, love! Yes! Life goes to all this trouble to present them with a beautiful moment—a bird singing, the smell of coffee, light through the window—and they spit on it! They snub the invitation to relish and enjoy what's on offer, just to focus on their own thoughts about what they did or didn't do in the past and what they will or won't do in the future. Do you not think that's disrespectful?"

"It kinda is, huh?" I said. "I guess we get so wrapped up in goals and accomplishments that we don't focus on the things that really matter, like family, kids, love—"

"No no no, you're still not getting it," she growled, cutting me off again. "That's not what this is about! Sure, loved ones are fine and good, but even if you focused on that you'd still be missing the gaps. If you focus on finding love, on spending enough time with everyone, on having kids and raising them, on making sure everyone in your life gets what they need from you and making sure you're getting what you need from them—that's still missing all those moments in between. The moments that don't have any stories to them, that don't depend on your thoughts about them. What about those? Are you there for them? Are you showing up to them?"

"Ohhh."

"You have all those gaps whether you have ten kids and a hundred friends or whether you live your whole life alone, and they're just as beautiful and worthy of appreciation either way. I'll tell you something for free lassy, I've lived more life in the last year here in this old folks' home than the eighty-three before it, because I finally stopped thinking about life and started living it. It finally clicked. After I came here I was sitting here looking at my hands, and it just washed over me: Oh, this is it, isn't it? This is where the joy really is. And so now I really relish each moment here. The hustle and bustle out there in the hallway, the chatter on my roommate's TV, the light through the curtains, the cotton on my skin. And I really relish them. I relish each and every moment here. And it's the happiest I've ever been."

And with that she gave my hand a squeeze and sent me on about my day.

I never saw her again. The next time I was back at the nursing home there was another woman in her bed. I didn't bother asking where she went; people don't leave that place because they found work overseas.

I expected to feel sad about that, but the sadness never came. All that came up was a deep, squishy gratitude. A deep, squishy gratitude that never really left.

Image by Adobe Stock

Printed in Great Britain
by Amazon